Old American Houses

OLD AMERICAN HOUSES

HOUSES

How to Restore, Remodel, and Reproduce Them

HENRY LIONEL WILLIAMS & OTTALIE K. WILLIAMS

DRAWINGS AND PHOTOGRAPHS BY THE AUTHORS EXCEPT WHERE NOTED

Bonanza Books   *New York*

*This edition published by Bonanza Books, a division
of Crown Publishers, Inc., by arrangement
with Coward-McCann, Inc.*

(F)

For

JOSEPHINE and LAURENCE FELLOWS

whose home is a shining example of old-time crafts-manship preserved and revivified with taste and understanding.

Preface

ELEVEN years ago we published a book on old houses bearing a somewhat similar, though less inclusive, title than the present volume. These two books are entirely unrelated, dealing with different aspects of the same subject. This new book is an attempt to present the history and origin of the small Colonial, and post-Colonial, houses in America as a help in understanding their design and construction. It discusses ways and means of preserving these early houses by restoring them to their original condition; by adapting them for modern living; by moving them to new sites; and by building replicas of them from salvaged materials that once formed other antique houses.

In this work we have received with gratitude the help and co-operation of many owners of such houses throughout the thirteen original States, who have allowed us to photograph and to sketch to our heart's content. Among those who have actively co-operated with us in the securing of information and in obtaining for us the entrée to especially intriguing houses are our good friends Jo and Larry Fellows, Rebecca and Fred Jones, Pat and Jack Knecht, Roberta Fay, and Muriel and Fred Baker.

We also owe a debt of thanks to those neighbors and friends who provided us with the opportunity to photograph some of the loveliness they have created. Their pictures are identified in the captions.

For their help in verifying some facts, and eliciting others, and, in general, offering a helping hand, we are grateful to Jack Connors of the Reardon Company; to Bert Little of the Society for the Preservation of New England Antiquities; John Cummings of the Bucks County Historical Society, and J. Paul Hudson of the National Park Service's Jamestown Museum.

Ottalie and Lionel Williams

Bloomfield, Conn.

7

This old house is now a charming and comfortable home.

Introduction

ANY old house that has been the cherished home of an American family for generations is a growing and vital thing. But it must be lived in and loved to be preserved; with age and neglect it can soon decay. The suns and the blizzards, the water below the ground and the heaving soil all do their best to destroy its fabric and hasten its return to Mother Earth. But the old-time craftsmen who hewed its timbers and shaped its stones knew well that they were building for posterity as well as the present generation of their day. They are all long gone but their handiwork remains as one of our cherished possessions—a link with our own and our country's past. And we who think of, and appreciate these things can never stand idly by to watch the simple beauty they created vanish into dust. To salvage such a house is a privilege. To do the job as it should be done; restoring where possible, remodeling where necessary without destroying the character that age and use have bestowed, is an opportunity to be seized in a spirit of dedication to a worthy cause.

Such a house, not too decrepit, can well be made into a comfortable home even by the demanding standards of today. Through proper restoration or remodeling, we can create within it backgrounds and atmosphere for the things we most enjoy without spoiling the essential old-time flavor of the house for someone else who may own it many years from now.

An authentic restoration, brought up to date by the incorporation of modern improvements such as weatherproofing, insulation, sanitary facilities, and kitchens has a far greater intrinsic value than one that is just another modern house built around an antique. The more that can be preserved of the original dwelling, the more interesting will the remodeled house be. And the more it will appeal to that growing class of Americans who value these irreplaceable examples of the handiwork of the men and women who lived and labored in them when the Republic was young and in the making.

To the uninitiated it may seem so easy to fake an interior to look like an old-time product. Actually, nothing is more difficult or calls for more detailed knowledge, if the old-time atmosphere and charm are to be preserved. The "cute" is but a short step from the quaint, and the ridiculous from the permissible. All of which does not mean that delightful results cannot be secured in the ruthless making-over of old-time houses.

They can, but unless the owner knows exactly what he is doing, he will have obtained that effect at the cost of losing everything he had to begin with. Worse still, another relic of our early civilization will have gone the way of all flesh.

A house that has been lived in for a century or two cannot help but acquire a well-used air. It has a familiar and settled "feel"; it displays the marks of use and the patina of age that a piece of antique furniture acquires. It has a special atmosphere compounded of old-fashioned moldings and wavy glass, bruised and dented woodwork, worn hearthstones, wide boards, windows of unusual proportions, a slight list here and there, smoke-aged fireplaces, narrow stairs, odd-shaped and small rooms, intriguing, tiny cupboards, and a general air of antiquity that cannot be faked.

Naturally, many such houses, after 150 to 200 years of use may also appear somewhat down-at-heel. But the important point is that this evidence of neglect can be wiped out without destroying everything else—if that impulse to make the old house look like a new one can be restrained. What we need to remember is that such houses can be brought up to date without robbing them of the features that make them attractive if only we take the trouble to find out how. No old-fashioned kitchen is improved with rows of ceiling cupboards and expanses of white enamel. No old house is better off for a modern, hotel-style bathroom any more than the old keeping-room is helped by being filled with modern furniture.

On the contrary, by careful study and planning, the kitchen can be equipped with the latest devices without offending the eye or robbing the room of its old-time look. Pine and paint can be used to subdue the glare and gleam, and surfaces may be substituted that are every bit as sanitary and much less arrogantly aseptic. Likewise, closets and cupboards can be provided, and remodeling judiciously effected without hiding steel girders in the ceilings.

Similarly, heating plants can be installed without sawing huge holes in the floors and walls, or cutting half way through the principal timbers. The house can be made safe to live in and protected to a high degree against fire, termites, and other destructive agents, and all without introducing a jarring note. All that is required is that the new owner realize such things are possible, and seek the help he needs in carrying them out. This book is designed to serve that need by indicating the principles involved and the historic reasons behind them.

Then there are those antique houses, large and small, that must be torn down or moved to make way for new highways or to escape a deteriorating neighborhood. Many of these, too, can be saved from annihilation by moving them or salvaging their parts. Here is the answer for those who want an old house for its atmosphere and associations, but cannot find one where they must live.

That it is possible today to re-create a house that looks as though it had grown on the site one hundred and fifty years ago is an idea much less fantastic than it may sound. It has been done many times, and to look at these replica houses no one would guess that they had not been built many generations ago. The photographs in these pages show how successfully this can be done. The *sine qua non* is old materials plus an appreciation, and knowledge, of what can be done with them—and how to

10

do it. Some of the practical information this book can supply; a natural instinct for the beautiful and good and right in such things, as well as the urge, will furnish the rest.

All of these things are discussed in turn in the following pages, beginning with a comprehensive view of the origins of the various types of houses and the metamorphoses they have undergone on the long journey toward becoming the ideal home of so many mid-twentieth-century Americans.

Apart from all this, a campaign of education and enlightenment among home seekers is urgently required. People who buy these old houses should have pointed out to them that they are the privileged custodians of national cultural assets that they have no moral right to fritter away and destroy. All over the East, and as far west toward the Mississippi as Ohio's Western Reserve, but particularly in New England, New York, Pennsylvania, Maryland, Virginia, and the Carolinas are whole villages and small towns of these houses dating from Colonial or Revolutionary days. They and the scattered country houses of the same types—Early American, Georgian, Greek Revival—give the countryside and rural neighborhoods a distinctive American character and charm.

In a day when there is so much ugliness and unrest in the world, these dwindling Old American Houses of wood, brick, and stone, should serve to remind us of a glorious past, and stand as a monument to craftsmen who bequeathed us a heritage of which we can justly be proud. The least that we can do is to help preserve these contributions to the finer elements of our national culture which can be copied but never replaced.

Contents

FULFILLMENT

by Frederick W. Branch

The man who built this house of mine
A hundred years ago
With Christian doors of smooth, clear pine
And chestnut timbers, row on row,
Whose oxen hauled the brick and lime,
Who squared the hearth's broad stone,
Could not foresee that Fate and Time
Would someday make it all my own.

Of course he knew that it would stay
Here, on its sturdy sills,
Long after his last Spring should lay
Her fragrant mornings on the hills.
So even if he did not know
Just who its owners were to be,
I'll still maintain that, years ago,
He planned and built this house for me.

Chapter I

Backgrounds and Origins

ANYONE who has ever fallen in love with a decrepit old house and yearned to possess it regardless of curling shingles and a list to the windward will recognize the truth of the aphorism that life is not ruled by reason but by sentiment.

Almost always the house that arouses such sentiments is of the smaller, intimate type, with more simple charm than architectural merit. Seemingly without exception, these are the unpretentious dwellings upon which successive generations of owners have left their mark and contributed to their character—houses built in a day when each carpenter and mason, having served a long apprenticeship, was a craftsman, and every owner built for posterity as well as for his own short span of life.

Throughout the thirteen original states and Ohio's Western Reserve such houses still survive in large numbers to become satisfying homes for today's Americans. Elsewhere throughout the country are many newer houses dating from the early nineteenth century, that, following the same plans and structural principles, have much of the charm of the older houses, often with a great deal more convenience.

Ordinarily, it is the age of these houses, the kind of living they represent, not their architectural features, that give them their value. And so if we can find a house that is architecturally pleasing as well as very old we have a treasure indeed. But so many of the very old houses available today have not survived the years unscathed. In the latter days their chief enemy was transient fashion, such as the fad for large window lights, for classical touches in the Georgian and Greek Revival eras, then for Victorian doors and hardware. Today that enemy is an equally insidious but utterly uninformed passion for the primitive. Even in these days of mass building, the demand for antique houses far exceeds the supply. Worse still, a high proportion of the old houses made over for present-day use have been robbed of much of their historic and antiquarian value through careless and ignorant "restoration." Ephemeral fashion and uninformed taste have wrought more destruction than time, termites, fire, and rot combined. Perhaps worst of all is the misguided passion for stripping things down to the bare bones in a wild effort to recapture an air of crude antiquity that exposes at the same time the "restorer's" ignorance.

Then, too, there are those who buy these old houses merely to obtain a substantial structure that can be modernized at less

A jewel of an early American center-chimney house, built about 1700—The historic Thompson house, Setauket, L. I. privately restored. (*Photo by Historic American Buildings Survey*)

cost (they hope) than building a new one. When once an old house has been given this thorough, modernizing treatment it is pretty much of a dead loss thereafter from the viewpoint of restoration. Unsympathetic tampering quickly destroys the air of antiquity—the very thing that gives these houses their value, financial as well as aesthetic, to those who know.

Therefore, if the old houses are to be restored, or even adapted for modern living, no change should be made without due thought backed by sound knowledge. Guesswork is not sufficient, and preconceived ideas need to be checked. For most of us, this involves serious study—or the turning over of the project to experts. Moreover, serious restoration calls for a certain state of mind—a sense of historic continuity that

enables us not only to appreciate these connecting links with the past and their value to the future generations, but to recognize the history and origin of their special features and evaluate the changes that mark their development over the years.

In dealing with any old house, then, the basic plan should be to salvage as much of it as possible, to reconstruct the lost or mutilated parts, using old-time materials, designs and finishes. Only in this way can we hope to recapture the spirit of the house and avoid the incongruous and the affected. One point, however, that needs to be kept in mind in deciding what is original and what is not, is that a house built in 1720 does not of necessity have to conform entirely to that period.

Houses that are lived in and are a part of

people's lives are themselves living, growing things, and normally they change with changing times. The decades and centuries of use and adaptation leave their mark upon them. Each house therefore presents, or should present, a picture of quiet, unconscious evolution that speaks of use and growth. A house that is tied in every respect to the year of its birth is an impersonal museum piece, and looks it. The aim of restoration, therefore, is to re-create not the exact original by destroying all that may have been added later, but to merge the old and the new in a smooth and friendly fashion that will give the whole an air of timelessness and persistent vitality. That is why the most satisfying plan of restoration inevitably calls for some firm, and not always happy, decisions. And these decisions must be based on something more than impulse and personal preference.

In restoration, too, we need to know not only what to expect, but to be able to recognize the reasons for certain peculiarities of construction and design that we will inevitably encounter. Even though we may never have cause to examine the structural details of a 17th Century house, the basic ideas and practices that such a house embodies may serve to explain otherwise puzzling details in later houses. Any antique house may be a puzzle as well as a challenge; few remain as they were originally built, and quite often we are faced with the necessity of deciding which feature is best sacrificed and which preserved.

For example, in one of our restoration jobs it was discovered that a large kitchen fireplace, complete with back-wall oven, existed behind the present small keeping-room fireplace. The small fireplace itself was around one hundred and seventy-five

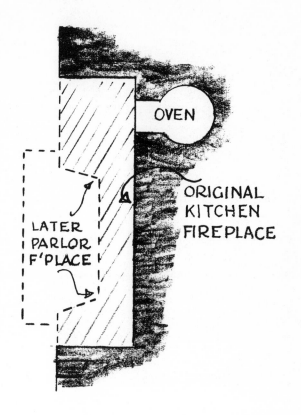

years old, and had nice paneling and attractive detail. There was also a kitchen fireplace, with its own brick oven behind the chimney in the later kitchen—and one eight-foot kitchen fireplace is usually enough in one house!

Uncovering the earlier large fireplace would have destroyed the small one and spoiled the room, besides affording a gamble on how much of the original fireplace had been mutilated in making the change. Furthermore, there would have been the added problem of draft control with the large, open-throated fireplace that the house really did not need. The owner very wisely decided not to tear out the small fireplace. As he said, he wanted a comfortable home, not merely a museum to live in.

A 16th-Century half-timbered English house of the kind the Colonists knew.

From the foregoing, then, it will be seen that a knowledge of house construction details is highly desirable before any restoration work is attempted. Many of the earlier houses were designed and built by carpenters and masons who worked by rule of thumb, but sometimes let their creative instincts get the better of them and introduced quirks of their own. Therefore, enough should be known about what to expect so that these interesting variations can be recognized for what they are and not ruthlessly eliminated as later changes made carelessly or in ignorance.

The first thing, therefore, in studying the subject of restoration is to achieve an understanding of how and why these houses are put together as they are; the basic characteristics of the various types, the reasons for their differences and peculiarities, and the variations that are likely to be found.

Obviously it is quite impossible here to detail all exceptions to the general rule likely to be encountered. It will be sufficient if common practice is detailed and certain principles established. When once we know what to expect we know what to look for. And when we do not find what we expect we are impelled to look further. That is one of the fascinations of old house restoration.

The Wooden House

For the backgrounds of the first American houses of the types that survive today,

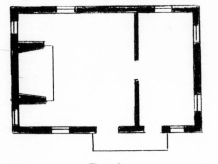

Dutch

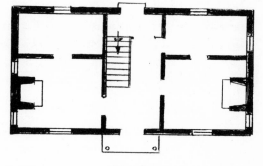

Dutch

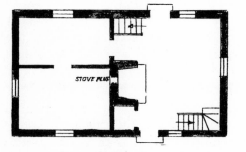

STOVE PLUG

Pennsylvania German

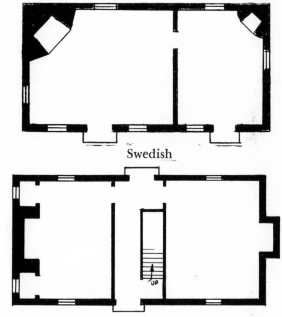

Swedish

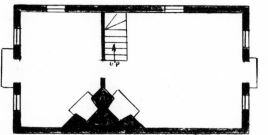

Swedish

Virginian

Here are seven house floor plans
of assorted national origins,

we have to go to Europe and in particular
England, the Netherlands and Germany.
The houses erected in the early days of the
new colonies—the second quarter of the
17th Century—when the settlers were firmly
established—were built by carpenters and
masons schooled in the old-country tradi-
tions. Very little that was developed before
the middle of the 18th Century was really
indigenous to the New World.

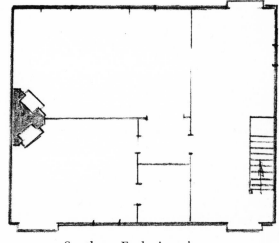

Southern Early American

One of the charms of the 18th Century houses is that they represent a natural and obvious development from more primitive habitations. Their design is logical and not contrived, nor based upon some new and revolutionary concept whose only claim to consideration is that it is "different." These wooden houses can trace their ancestry from the 8th Century or earlier cruck construction.

How small houses acquired vertical walls—the development from the early cruck construction.

The crucks consisted of a pair of curved uprights put together, wishbone fashion. Two or more pairs of them were spaced, usually, sixteen feet apart to support a ridge-pole. The result was a tent-like structure that was covered with rush or basket-work and sod. The next stage of development was to use tie-beams across the upper part of the crucks. These extended out on either side, and on them was laid a longitudinal timber on which the feet of the rafters could rest. These longitudinals made it possible to build vertical walls under them; the walls in turn offered space for wider rooms, and did away with the need for the legs of the crucks.

By supporting the ridge-pole on a vertical post resting on each tie-beam center (which now actually became a floor beam), the roof became a self-supporting truss, and the upper parts of the crucks likewise served no useful purpose thereafter. The king-post

From cruck to kingpost—the origin of small-house roof framing.

An English 14th-Century cottage, utilizing crucks and tie beams—the second stage of cruck design.

roof truss had arrived. Later came a variation of this, using two posts instead of one and connecting their tops with a tie-beam between the rafters. This afforded more clear floor space in the roof. It was—and is—called the queen-post truss, and both queen-post and king-post trusses are used, with variations, in all the houses we are going to talk about whether they are of stone, wood, or brick. The rest was merely a matter of building walls to support this integrated roof structure.

The walls now consisted of two or more posts, depending on the size, with lighter posts and rails between them to support the wall material, and frame the doors and windows.

The queen post roof made possible the use of floor space where the roof was highest under the ridge.

An early English "saltbox" house
with Elizabethan half-timbering.

The Half-timbered House

This truss-roof and post-wall form of construction was developed, in the 14th and 15th Centuries, into the Tudor half-timbered house. Here the wall spaces were filled in first with withes and clay and later with bricks, often laid in ornamental patterns, but without mortar. Later, these brick-filled walls were sealed with plaster, whitewashed to help resist the weather. Some of this type were among the first houses erected in the Virginia Colony.

These houses were two stories tall, with a high-peaked roof. The reason for the high peak was that in all these early houses, storage space was badly needed, and best secured by laying a rough floor over the wind beams, as the roof ties were called. This is why many of these houses had windows or doors in the peaks of the gables. Heavy corner braces were used in the gables on both floors. Curved braces between principal rafters and purlins were an important part of the roof structure. But, to us perhaps, the most interesting part of the building is the overhang, since we inherited it.

This overhang was achieved by extending the second floor joists, which ran from front to back, out over the first-floor frame. This could readily be done because the main vertical timbers—in particular the corner posts—did not extend in one piece above the first floor ceiling height. In other words, the second floor was really a separate structure.

In England the overhang was often built out both front and back of the house. This

24

This frame of an Elizabethan half-timbered house shows how the overhang was secured.

most logical reason lies in the fact that the overhang stiffened the horizontal timbers of the upper floor. The weight of the upper floor, or floors, was carried on the ends of these beams. This cantilever effect tended to bend the beams upward and so stiffened them, eliminating sag, and reducing vibration. It also allowed smaller timbers to be used. When these floor beams were replaced with shorter joists, supported at the middle of the room by a large beam called a summer beam (or bressummer), the need for the overhang was eliminated.

Though some of the earliest houses built in America were based on the Elizabethan half-timbered house of 16th-Century England, the open walls would not withstand the rigorous climate here, especially in the North-east. The solution was to cover them with something more substantial such as wooden siding or clapboards. Using a nailed-on covering for the frame and eliminating the brick filling rendered it unnecessary to make the frame in the form of panels (square openings between the beams and posts) to hold the bricks. This simplified the whole structure. Apart from corner braces, the house frame could then be constructed principally of vertical timbers—large ones to form the main frame, smaller ones to support the outer and inner wall coverings. And so the braced frame that was to play such a large part in American wooden house building for almost two hundred years came into being.

was done by simply extending the first floor ceiling beams a couple of feet beyond the lower walls. In larger houses, these beams did not extend right across the lower part, but were jointed into crosswise and lengthwise main beams instead. This meant that the floor beams could be laid at any angle and extended in any direction—even diagonally at the corners—and the overhang extended beyond the front, sides, and back if desired.

The purpose of the overhang has never been fully explained, though all sorts of hypotheses have been advanced. To us the

A 16th-Century remodelling of a 15th-Century English cottage interior. The resemblance to 17th-Century American design is remarkable. *(Photo, Homes & Gardens, London)*

Chapter II

Braced Frames and Masonry

ALL of the American wooden houses with which we are concerned here are of the braced-frame type. This means that they are built on a frame of massive timbers jointed and pegged together and kept square with stiff braces in the vertical angles.

This frame is used regardless of the type of house and location of the chimney or chimneys. It also composes the backbone of ells, leantos, and extensions. However, in examining the braced frame it will simplify matters—especially that of nomenclature—if we consider a specific type: the central-chimney wooden house, of which there are so very many.

The typical two-story, central-chimney Colonial house, one room deep, is built on an eight-post frame. First of all there is the sill which rests on a stone or brick foundation. These timbers are often 7x10 inches or larger, laid on their broad side and jointed at the corners and ends of each timber.

In the center of the foundation is the massive stone chimney, often eight to twelve feet square at the base. If the house sits directly on the ground, another pair of sills runs from the front to the rear, one each side of the chimney. If, as is more usual, there is a cellar, these inside sills change their names to cellar girts. They are then partially supported by the chimney masonry instead of on a foundation wall.

The eight posts, all of which run the full height of the building walls, consist of four corner posts and four intermediate ones, called chimney posts, at the ends of the girts. While the end sills and the girts support the ground-floor joists, another set of horizontal timbers carries the second-floor joists. These main timbers, extending around the frame at second-floor level, are the first-floor front, rear, end, and chimney girts respectively. The roof of the house is carried on the top set of timbers. These consist of a front and rear plate, and the second-floor end girts or plates.

In moderate-sized houses, one room deep, these timbers are sufficient to carry the floor joists. On the other hand, where the rooms are large, shorter and stiffer joists are called for. This problem is solved by the introduction of extra timbers called summer beams. These timbers usually run parallel to the front of the house, from the end girts to the chimney girts, half way from front to rear. These summers are the most massive timbers in the house, since they have to be notched on both sides to carry the ends of two sets of floor joists. The other ends of these joists are notched into the front and rear girts. In some houses there is also a summer beam in the cellar ceiling, but this is not usually necessary since the floor joists can be made much larger, not having to be hidden in a ceiling.

How a braced frame was put together in sections on the ground.

The summers, being so large that they usually project through the ceilings, are made a decorative feature by having their corners chamfered or carved. In other instances they are entirely hidden in the thickness of the ceiling. Still later ones may be partially hidden by the plastered ceiling and enclosed in a beaded casing. By checking for the presence or absence of a summer beam it is possible to tell which way the joists run, regardless of how many layers of flooring have been applied.

In houses that have rooms behind the chimney, there will be another set of four posts, with a rear sill, and the end and chimney girts tied into them. When a second set of rooms is added to a house that originally was only one room deep, the original rear plate becomes a second summer in the top-floor ceiling. In the larger houses also there may be two summers in each floor, and in Massachusetts the summer beams usually run from front to rear of the house. Wherever there is a summer beam it will be found that the timbers supporting it are proportionately heavier.

Frame braces, usually 2x6 or 3x6, are tenoned and pegged into corner and chim-

Erecting the braced frame sections and pegging them together.

ney posts. The braces may run up to the girt or plate, or down to the girt or sill. In many early houses they are visible on the interior; in others they are plastered over.

To support the wall coverings and form the interior partitions, vertical members called studs are tenoned into the upper and lower frame members. Since they carry no load, these studs are usually no larger than 2½x3 or 3x3 inches in section. As a rule they are spaced twenty to twenty-four inches on centers.

In a great many of these houses, even well into the 20th Century, heavy planks were used both for the outside walls and interior partitions in place of studs. These planks may be one and one-eighth to two inches thick, of oak or chestnut, and twelve inches or more wide. They usually are spaced an inch or more apart, and either pinned or nailed to the sills, girts and plates. In the early houses the planks may extend in one piece from sill to plate. In some instances the sills are rabbeted to receive the feet of the planks.

In the case of end-chimney wooden houses, the arrangement of the frame timbers is substantially the same though the

29

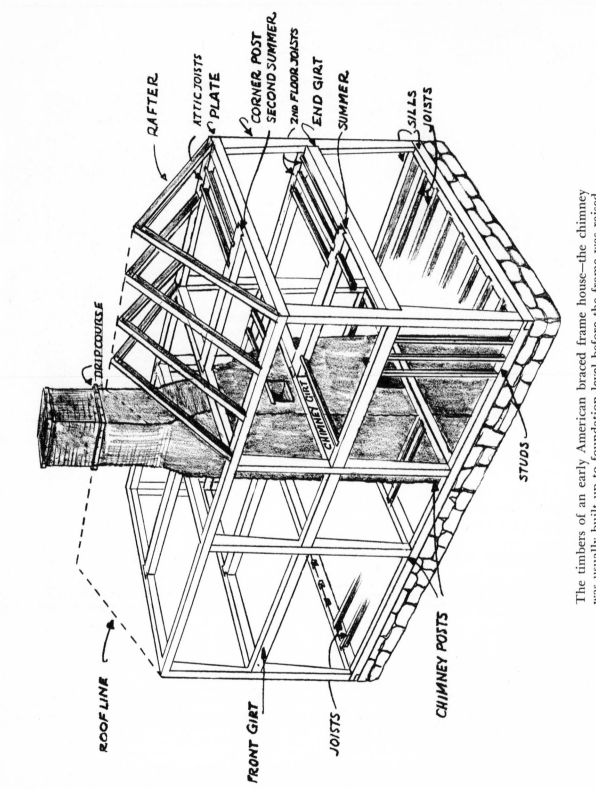

RAFTER

ATTIC JOISTS

PLATE

CORNER POST

SECOND SUMMER

2ND FLOOR JOISTS

END GIRT

SUMMER

SILLS

JOISTS

DRIPCOURSE

CHIMNEY GIRT

STUDS

ROOF LINE

FRONT GIRT

JOISTS

CHIMNEY POSTS

The timbers of an early American braced frame house—the chimney was usually built up to foundation level before the frame was raised.

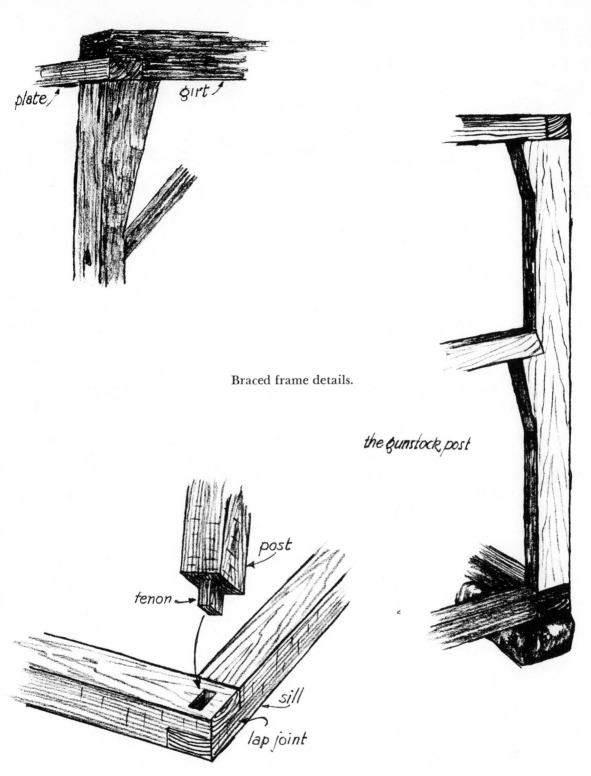

plate

girt

Braced frame details.

the gunstock post

post

tenon

sill

lap joint

31

hewn overhang

The hewn overhang.

upper front girt

The framed overhang.

names of the individual posts and beams will vary according to their location. And since most of the end-chimney houses have central halls in place of a chimney, the same posts and girts will remain.

The Overhang

In making the transition from the Tudor half-timbered house to the braced-frame construction, the overhang was at first retained. This overhang, which was of the framed variety, was confined to the front of the house and extended about two feet out over the lower part of the building. There was, however, an important difference in the frame construction to permit of this overhang. In the case of the half-timbered frame, the second floor was built on top of the first floor beams. In the braced-frame, the rear posts were carried up the full two stories in one piece; only the front posts were cut off at second floor level to allow for the overhang.

A second deviation from the Tudor practice was the introduction of a vestigial over-

hang at the ends of the building. This "hewn" overhang was secured by using extra heavy corner posts and cutting away their lower part so that the upper ends projected two to six inches beyond it. The horizontal end timbers (the end girts) were framed to these posts so that they supported the upper walls slightly beyond the face of the first-story walls.

The framed overhang, which provided an opportunity for forming carved drops or "pendills" on the lower extensions of the corner and chimney posts, had disappeared from American architecture by 1700. Later houses had merely a hewn overhang of a few inches, sometimes repeated also at the roof or third-story level. While you are not likely to acquire an antique house with a framed overhang, a great many reproductions of this type have been built in recent years, a tribute to their attractive appearance.

By the early 1700s, as we have seen, the framed overhang was largely forgotten, and two-story houses were mostly built with all

Detail of a hewn overhang in an early 18th-Century house.

posts formed of single timbers running from sill to plate.

A great many Dutch- or Flemish-style houses were built of wood in early Colonial days. In these houses the frames were constructed of heavy timbers, as in New England, but there were important differences. The tendency was to use heavy timbers throughout—large joists and fewer of them, extending from front to rear of the house. These were covered with floors of heavy planks one and one-half inches or more in thickness. Summer beams were entirely absent, because the heavy joists made them unnecessary.

This variation in framing will also be found in the Dutch and Flemish houses that were built with two or three walls of masonry and one, or two, of wood. This type of house, also occasionally encountered in New England, required a complete braced frame to take care of the wooden walls. The masonry walls, on the other hand, could support the horizontal timbers without the need for posts.

Wall Coverings

Wooden houses in America have been covered with clapboard siding since the 17th Century. Such clapboards were used on medieval English houses, and were called weatherboards. They were also common in Holland. It is believed that the few half-timbered houses built in the American colonies also were clapboarded over the wall filling.

The early clapboards were of oak, cedar, or pine, and ranged from five and one-half to eight inches wide. Being split from a round log, they were tapered in section from about three-sixteenths of an inch at the thin edge to three-eighths or one-half inch at the butt. Lengths varied from four to six feet, according to the spacing of the studs which were usually two feet on centers, one board being nailed to two, or three, studs.

Somewhat thicker clapboards with very little taper were also used in the early days. When these were applied to the studs they were bevelled at the ends to form an overlapping joint—something that could not be done with the featheredged clapboards. This practice was continued till about 1800. This type of clapboard, dating from the early 1700s, was often made with a bead along the lower edge. Those we have had the opportunity of examining have all been six inches wide or over, and some of them dated from the middle of the 18th Century when this practice was apparently revived. These should not be confused with the still later rectangular beaded siding that was rabbeted at the top edge to receive half the thickness of the board above it.

In most instances the clapboards were finished against 1x3 to 1x6 corner boards. These boards may be plain or finished with a

33

Beaded clapboards provide an extra shadow line that adds to the attractiveness of the white exterior. (*Courtesy Mr. & Mrs. Philip Van Wyck*)

narrow bead. There are, however, some 17th Century examples of clapboards mitered at the corners. The Clemence House at Manton, R.I. is an example, as is the Paul Revere House, and the House of Seven Gables.

From about 1740 on, there was a vogue in some areas for graduating the exposure of the clapboards. The depth of each clapboard exposed to view gradually increased from the bottom row up, usually reaching maximum exposure somewhere near the tops of the first-floor windows. In some instances the width of the individual clapboards varies so that the overlap remains constant; in other cases the boards are all the same width and the lap varies. This variation raises a question as to whether the idea was to provide extra protection where it was most needed or was simply a decorative feature. The fact that in many instances only the front walls of the houses were thus treated suggests that it was merely a matter of appearance.

Other early siding consisted of sawn boards twelve to eighteen inches wide and three-quarter-inch thick, fastened horizontally to the studs. These had either a beveled or rabbeted joint, and often included a bead at the lower edge. Somewhat narrower boards, seven-eighth-inch thick were rabbeted at the upper edge and beaded at the lower one. When installed, with the usual clapboard overlap, the beaded edge projected beyond the board beneath it, producing a shadow line and giving the appearance of very wide clapboards. The flat board finishes were apparently more popular among the Dutch and Flemish, and in the Southern States than elsewhere, especially where they were protected by deep eaves, pent roofs, or porches.

According to some authorities, the use of shingles for siding originated with the Dutch on Long Island. If this is so, the idea must have caught on rapidly, for many houses on Nantucket adopted it before 1700. The 17th-Century Jethro Coffin house on the Island is a notable example. Siding shingles also were made in southern Connecticut in 1639!

Many of these early shingles were of white pine, up to three feet long and ten inches wide. They were split rough, then finished slightly with a draw-knife. Having the natural grooves on the surface they shed water better than the smooth sawn ones—a fact that undoubtedly accounts for their long life. Some of them, incidentally, were given an occasional coat of whitewash in their earlier years.

The Ogden House, Fairfield, Conn. is a fine example of an early American "saltbox." (*Photo by Historic American Buildings Survey*)

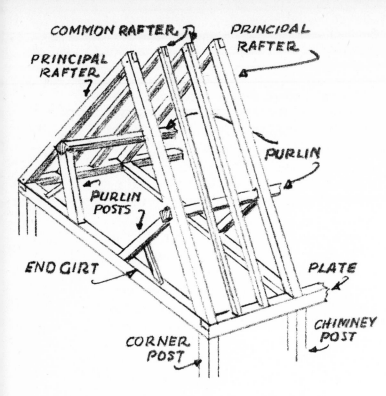

COMMON RAFTER

PRINCIPAL RAFTER

PRINCIPAL RAFTER

PURLIN

PURLIN POSTS

END GIRT

PLATE

CORNER POST

CHIMNEY POST

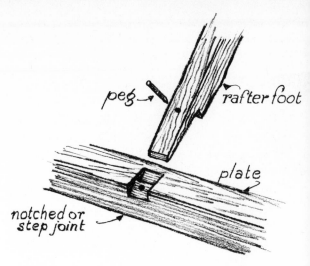

peg

rafter foot

plate

notched or step joint

Details of roof framing for center-chimney house.

How a rafter foot was jointed to the plate. Fig. 25.

Roofs

There is a great variation in the framing of old-time roofs, much of it individual rather than chronological. Perhaps the most general and simplest arrangement consists of a series of common rafters, with no ridge board, and sometimes no collar beam or ties. In this common-rafter system, the pairs of rafters are all of equal size and evenly spaced. This means that they all take an equal share of the load. The size of these rafters varies considerably and depends both on the length and on the presence or absence of collar beams. This also affects the spacing.

Two kinds of rafters are used in roof construction—common rafters and principal rafters. The common rafters are usually fairly light (perhaps 3x4), and closely spaced, say three feet on centers. Principal rafters are heavier and more widely spaced. Quite often several pairs of common rafters will be installed between each two pairs of principal rafters in order to provide a strong roof and adequate all-over support for the roof covering. Each of these varieties is described in detail.

In section, the common rafters may range from 3x4 to 5x7, though quite irregular and sometimes tapering from top to bottom. Usually, the older the house the heavier the rafters, and more often than not they were laid on their broader sides. There are also large variations in the quality of the workmanship. In some smaller houses the rafters may be simply rough poles dressed on the upper side only. Such rafters, however, are not necessarily older than those that are sawn or dressed all over with an ax.

Difference also may be noted in the methods used in joining the pairs of rafters at the ridge, and in jointing them to the plates. If there is a ridge board—something found more often after 1800 than before it—the rafter ends will be cut to fit flat against it, and spiked together through it. In earlier

36

Typical jointing of rafter foot and plate in early 18th-Century "saltbox."

roofs, the almost universal method was to halve the joint, or cut a barefaced tenon, and drive a treenail through the two.

The commonest method of joining the rafter foot to the plate was by means of a stepped joint (Fig. 25). In late work, however, the rafter might be cut to rest on the plate and be held with spikes. Where the rafter extends beyond the plate to form overhanging eaves, the stepped joint would be used, with the plate's outer corner cut away slightly.

The function of the collar beam or tie was to prevent the rafters bowing inward at the center with the weight of snow or the wind pressure—hence the English name for them: wind beams. Since this timber was usually firmly jointed to the rafters it also helped to prevent the rafter feet spreading and pushing outward on the walls. In such cases it would act as a tension member,

and that, undoubtedly, is why some of these joints are halved dovetails or pinned mortises and tenons (Fig. 27). On occasion a collar beam is found with no dovetail or peg, indicating that the carpenter used it as a compression member only, and realized it could not come apart because of the weight of the roof on the rafters.

In some of the common-rafter roofs, the collar beams are replaced by longitudinal timbers running the length of the roof to support the rafters at midpoint. These members are called purlins, and may be 6x6 or larger. In some instances these heavy purlins are supported by posts framed into the four girts at an angle so that they are at right angles to the rafters. The posts, in turn, are supported by smaller struts.

Other roofs may be framed with four or more pairs of principal rafters, with two or more pairs of common rafters between each two pairs of principals. The principal rafters then carry the purlins, and the common rafters are pinned to it. This purlin usually is carried around the ends (across the gables), being framed into the end pairs of principal rafters so that they form a rigid truss. Such a roof frequently has corner braces between the end rafters and the purlins.

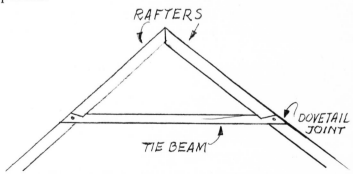

How the beam was jointed to resist both roof pressures and spreading. Fig. 27.

A "windbeam" in the gable of an English stone house.

In roofs composed of principal rafters, a large number of very small purlins may be used—or what seem to be purlins. These "purlins" may be as small as 1½ x 2½ inches, and let in flush with the faces of the rafters. If the purlins are fairly close together it may be assumed that their original purpose was to hold the roof covering. Some such roofs today are shingled, but the use of very narrow purlins for this is definitely not good design; they would not stand very many nailings! In such cases it may be—in the case of a 17th Century house—that the "purlins" are really thatch poles, a relic of very early times. In other cases they may have served to hold clay tiles, such tiles having a hook or lip formed behind their top edge to act as an anchor. When heavier purlins are used, even with principal rafters, they are always on the underside of such rafters and pegged to them. In such cases the roof is intended to be covered with boards laid horizontally, to which the roof covering would be nailed. In other roofs, where heavy purlins are halved into the top faces of the rafters, the roofing boards (commonly referred to as "roofers") would be installed vertically from plate to ridge. Incidentally, many of the purlin roofs also have a purlin at the ridge where it acts as a ridge board. This also would be let in flush with the rafters on one side of the ridge.

In many of the early houses, the upper floor was often used for storage as well as for sleeping. And quite often a lack of suf-

TILE LUG

PA. CLAY TILE

Clay tile with lip for hanging over light purlins or "thatch poles."

ficient storage space made it necessary to install a partial floor over the roof tie-beams. We have noted this particularly in the case of Dutch and Flemish houses, two rooms deep, where the roof is particularly massive and steep. In such buildings—especially the masonry ones—there might also be a door in the gable for the hoisting of grain, etc., to the top floor. Sometimes this door had been replaced with a window in the later 18th Century. It is also in these Dutch-style houses that there is occasionally found a system of auxiliary braces supporting the rafters. One such an arrangement, an original feature of the house, is illustrated. (Fig. 30).

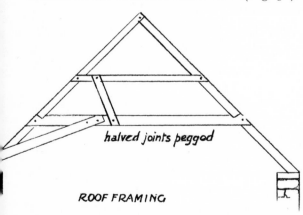

halved joints pegged

ROOF FRAMING

The use of floored-over roof timbers often called for auxiliary supports. Fig. 30.

The Gambrel Roof

The gambrel roof, with its double slope each side of the ridge, achieved a certain popularity throughout the colonies for the simple reason that it provided extra upstairs accommodations at little added cost. In some areas, such as those populated by Dutch, English, Flemish, and Swedish colonists, its use was a matter of tradition. In others, the gambrel sometimes replaced an originally peaked roof to provide more second-floor space—a much more acceptable solution than the ugly running dormer!

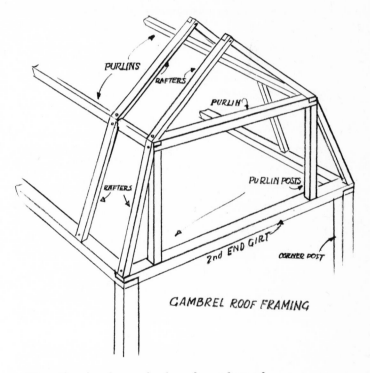

PURLINS

RAFTERS

PURLIN

RAFTERS

PURLIN POSTS

2nd END GIRT

CORNER POST

GAMBREL ROOF FRAMING

How the simple gambrel roof was framed.

In other instances, a peaked roof was made more commodious by converting only half of it—usually the front—to the gambrel form. There are also quite a few leanto houses with the front roof of gambrel shape.

Here is a happy marriage of gambrel and "saltbox" leanto roofs—providing much needed headroom at the front of the house attic. (*Courtesy Mr. George C. Lyon*)

Wherever changes such as this to the original roof are suspected, the junction between roof timbers and the plates or girts may tell the story. Incidentally, all such conversions that we have encountered thus far date from the late 18th or early 19th Centuries.

While there is a great variety of gambrel shapes, some of them do serve as an indica-

tion of their national origin. Six basic types are illustrated. (Fig. 33). Those termed English are of two contrasting shapes: a high-peaked gambrel, and a lower, flatter one. The latter were said to have been introduced into England in the early 17th Century from Holland by the Dutch engineers who helped drain and dike the fens of East Anglia. The steeper type is a relic of Tudor days, and essentially English. As usual with such innovations they were modified somewhat in the process of transplantation, as were those introduced into America during the last quarter of the 17th Century. The fact that some gambrels have an attractive appearance (those with longer, less steep, lower sections) while others do not, may be due to the difficulties of maintaining proportions for different spans while providing head clearance inside. This is why gambrels on houses one room deep usually seem less pleasing to the eye. If the height were reduced in proportion to the spread, the room inside could be used only by dwarfs!

The most attractive gambrel of all is that principally found in one and a half story houses of Long Island and Northern New Jersey and commonly attributed to the Dutch. This "Dutch" gambrel is to many people the sole identifying feature of a house

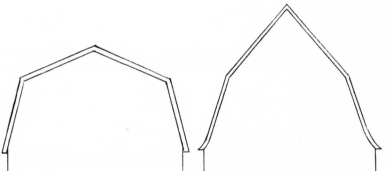

(a) English, 17th Century.

(b) North Carolina & Connecticut.

(c) English 17th Century, North Carolina & Maryland.

Six basic types of gambrel roof shapes—their proportions

style popularly called Dutch Colonial. Actually, these gambrels which have a short upper slope of about 22°, and a sweeping lower one of around 45°, are not Dutch but Flemish. These Flemish roofs are distinguished by their eaves that extend in a graceful curve two feet or more beyond the front and rear walls of the house. The truly Dutch Colonial has a peaked roof, usually with end chimneys. The Flemish style is discussed in greater detail in the pages devoted to masonry houses.

Houses of Stone and Brick

Masonry houses of small and medium size were built in the colonies from the earliest times. Only in New England, where there were extensive forests and a climate that wood could well withstand, did the wooden house predominate for long.

No doubt the fact that the settlers for the most part hailed from English counties where wood was the favored building material had a great deal to do with this. On the other hand, the Massachusetts Bay group counted among their members a number of brickmakers who were very soon exercising their trade. Furthermore, in spite of the fact that lime to make mortar was far from plentiful, a number of stone houses were

put up in the 17th Century. Perhaps the most famous of these is the Whitfield House at Guilford, Connecticut, erected in 1639. The walls of this house are of ledge stone set in a mortar of clay and pulverized oyster shells. There are also documentary references to a number of other such houses long since demolished.

One important New England brickmaking center was Medford, Massachusetts, which started production in 1629. In those early days the bricks were used largely for chimneys and bake ovens, but several important brick houses were erected well before the end of the 17th Century. One of the most noted of these is the still-existing two and a half story Peter Tufts house which dates from 1675. A large number of brick houses were also put up in Boston in the late 17th and early 18th Centuries, plus some notable ones in the New Haven area. But not until the Georgian era—around 1740—did the use of brick become widespread throughout these states.

From the earliest days bricks were highly favored as a building material in Maryland, parts of Pennsylvania, and particularly in the Virginia Colony. By 1611 Virginia had its first brickyard operating, and within the next thirty years a number of brick man-

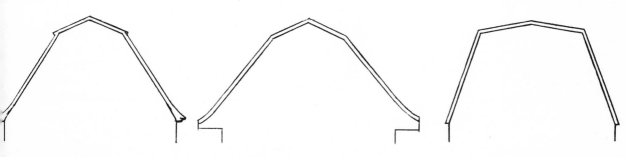

(d) New England & South Carolina.

(e) Dutch (Flemish) 17th Century.

(f) Swedish.

often change with the depth of the house. Fig. 33.

The Library at Middle Haddam, Connecticut is a delightful example of gambrel proportions.

French Huguenot interpretation of Dutch door with double transom.

sions had been erected. As bricks became more generally available, and presumably cheaper, their use was extended to farm houses and small urban dwellings.

Meanwhile the Dutch were putting up their stone houses in New Amsterdam and along the Hudson valley. Actually, brick was the favored building material of the Dutch—as it was in Holland—but in most localities in which they settled they were forced to use stone. An important exception was the Albany area where bricks were available in quantity. Where bricks were scarce, or were too high in price for general use, the Dutch sometimes used them to build the front wall of their stone houses or perhaps merely to frame the windows and doors.

Far too often confused with these Dutch houses are the Flemish stone houses of northern New Jersey and parts of lower New York. Like the Flemish houses of wood, indigenous to Long Island, these stone houses are distinguished by the sweeping eaves that extend in a graceful curve two feet or more beyond the front and rear walls. In the later 18th-Century houses these eaves were sometimes extended far enough to form a porch roof supported by posts. These were all originally one and a half story houses, two rooms deep, and when the gambrel roof was adopted to increase the usable second-floor space, the famous "Dutch" gambrel profile resulted.

Naturally, the Flemish houses in New Jersey were built of Bergen red sandstone. The very early ones were built with a mortar of yellow clay mixed with cow hair. In the later 18th Century, lime mortar was used, the white joints providing an interesting contrast with the red stone. Some of

A Hudson Valley stone house (1705) showing beam irons in gable. Louis DuBois House, New Paltz, New York. (*Photo by New York Historical Society*)

the houses with clay mortar also had their weather-washed joints pointed with the white lime-mortar, a sign of fashionable modernity.

In Maryland and eastern Pennsylvania, brick was the commoner building material, but in some areas of western Pennsylvania the German settlers made good use of the available fieldstone, as they did the ledge-stone of Bucks, Lebanon, Chester, and Lancaster Counties.

In all of these areas the 18th Century saw a rapid expansion of building throughout the colonies, and the development of types of houses having pronounced local characteristics. In some areas wooden houses were put up alongside stone and brick ones; in other places stone or brick—and sometimes both—were combined with wood. In dealing with any house that incorporates one or more walls of masonry, the important thing today is the construction and its effect on restoration and remodeling.

The typical stone and brick houses were built substantially, with stone walls two feet thick, or more, and brick walls only slightly thinner. The heavy horizontal framing timbers were then supported in recesses or on

43

A Pennsylvania stone house with pent roofs.

corbels and ledges. Very often the gable and roof timbers would be secured to the masonry wall by means of "beam irons"—heavy bolts terminating in decorative iron braces on the outside of the gable walls.

The masonry gable might extend upward as far as the roof ridge, or all walls may end at the plates and the gables be covered with wood. In some few instances, the masonry ends at the tops of the gable windows as in the Dutch-style houses erected by the French Huguenots in the Hudson Valley area.

Occasionally houses were built with masonry gable walls enclosing the usual braced frame so that they had wooden walls front and rear. In other instances, three walls might be of masonry and the fourth of wood. In the former case, the house would probably include a complete frame of timbers. With only one wooden wall the chances are that there would be no timber posts adjacent to the stone work, but only as a part of the wooden wall.

Whether a house was of wood, brick, or stone, one notable feature was the tendency everywhere except pre-Georgian New England to favor houses with end chimneys, even when there was only one fireplace. In the earlier and smaller houses, the end chimney with its kitchen fireplace might

44

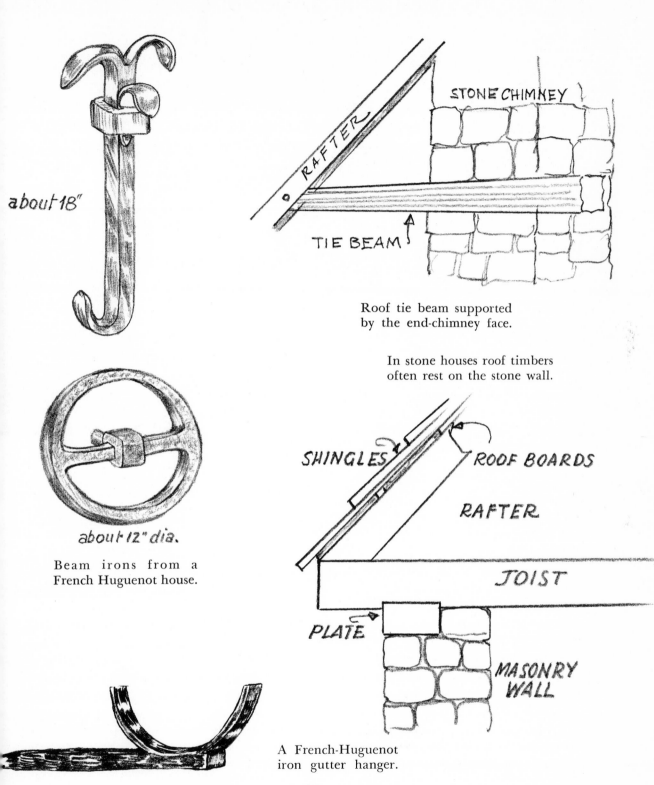

about 18"

Beam irons from a
French Huguenot house.

about 12" dia.

STONE CHIMNEY

RAFTER

TIE BEAM

Roof tie beam supported
by the end-chimney face.

In stone houses roof timbers
often rest on the stone wall.

SHINGLES

ROOF BOARDS

RAFTER

JOIST

PLATE

MASONRY
WALL

A French-Huguenot
iron gutter hanger.

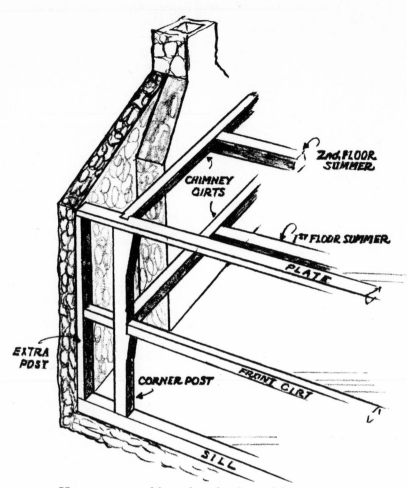

How a stone gable-end and a braced-frame were
joined together in the Rhode Island stone-ender.

well occupy most of the gable wall. This
sometimes resulted in one entire gable of a
wooden house being built of masonry.

This is what happened in the case of the
famed "stone-enders" of Rhode Island. Both
stone and lime were available there, but
houses of wood were apparently preferred,
and the central chimney was not looked
upon with particular favor. The result was
a one-room plan with a very large fireplace
that occupied a good deal of the one end
wall. Instead of doubling the floor area by
adding another room which would have a
fireplace back-to-back with the original one,
the new room was placed behind the existing one. This had the effect of incorporating two fireplaces side by side in the same
gable. The flues of these fireplaces were
run together into one chimney. Usually the
added room formed a leanto to house the
kitchen, so that the house had a saltbox
shape with an end chimney. The rest of the
house was built around the usual braced
frame.

46

Chapter III

The Chimney in the Middle

THE reasons for building so many wooden houses in the center-chimney style are quite logical. A large fireplace for cooking, dyeing, candlemaking and other home activities was a prime necessity in those days. Other rooms needed fireplaces for heating. Since a substantial masonry structure was needed for the large fireplace and ovens, and that fireplace called for a chimney extending well above the roof, it was but common sense to incorporate the smaller fireplaces in the large one and use the same flue. Furthermore, arranging the rooms around the chimney not only conserved heat but made possible a fireplace for each room both upstairs and down.

The same form of chimney structure which could be added to as desired then served the one-room, two-room, and four-room-plan houses; the two story, and the leanto types as well. The central chimney therefore was ideal for the owner who contemplated enlarging his house by degrees from one room to four or more. This massive pile of masonry also formed a solid and substantial core for the frame house, providing support for the chimney girts and adding rigidity to the entire frame.

In practically all of the center-chimney houses, the chimney structure is built of stone—sometimes of quarried stone, sometimes of fieldstone. In the majority of the earliest chimneys, the stones of the base are laid "dry", only the upper parts having clay or clay-plus-hair joints. When fieldstones were used it was common practice to insert old timbers as binders in the base. A great many of these chimney bases are not filled with rubble but are left hollow. There may even be an opening in the side of the base leading to this hollow space or vault. The base is often made circular inside, like a well, and covered with a heavy, flat stone. In later examples the interior might be of brick. Brick also was used to form an arched top to the base. In still other instances there might be an arched passageway right through the chimney.

The purpose of the opening into the chimney base is a matter of conjecture; some say that the space was used as a larder to keep food cool; others that it served as storage for the wood ashes used for making lye. This is quite possible since some hearths had a hole into which ashes could be raked. Presumably this hole led to the hollow chimney base, and was later done away with.

In some instances large timbers are incorporated in the chimney base to carry the

47

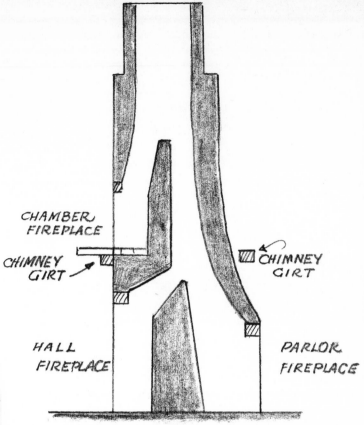

CHAMBER FIREPLACE

CHIMNEY GIRT

CHIMNEY GIRT

HALL FIREPLACE

PARLOR FIREPLACE

Most early central chimneys are of stone set in clay like this one. (*Courtesy Miss Janie Pierce*)

The core of many early American braced frame houses was the central chimney with fireplaces. Fig. 41.

The flues of a central chimney stack terminate in an open flue above the attic floor.

Arch in a Pennsylvania stone chimney base.

chimney girts on their ends, and at the back of the chimney to support the fireplace cradle. In other cases, some of the stones projected to serve the same purpose. The fireplace cradles often consisted of several short timbers leaning outward from the chimney base, their tops resting against a beam or floor joist. The space was then filled with large stones on which the hearth could be laid. (Fig. 45.) Sometimes smaller stones were used, held in the cradle by boards laid on the supports. For fireplaces at the sides of the chimney, the hearthstones would rest on the girts and may extend over the joists. In many houses the small fireplaces had no front hearth at all!

To support second-floor fireplaces, walls of stone or brick were occasionally built up from the tapering shoulders of the stack. (Fig. 41.) Where all the fireplaces were on the main floor, the flues would terminate in the open chimney at first-floor ceiling level. With fireplaces on the second floor there would be a common flue from the

second-floor ceiling height. In either case a vertical flagstone might be set across the main chimney to separate the two sets of flues for a short distance above their junction.

Cellar fireplaces are not common, but some very large ones do exist, mostly in later houses. These may have been slave kitchens, or used simply for such messy operations as lard rendering or lye making.

While many of the very early chimneys, and some of the later ones, were made of stone throughout, more were topped off with bricks set in lime mortar. Sometimes the stone portion would end at attic-floor level; others would extend up as far as the ridge before changing to brick. In other instances the top of a stone chimney was later taken down and brick substituted.

Where a leanto was added to the house, a new fireplace would be built at the back of the original central chimney. In some cases the flue for the new fireplace would be cut into the existing stack above the main-floor ceiling level. More often, a new flue would be built the full height of the stack to the rear of the chimney. The upper part of the chimney would then either be rebuilt to incorporate the extra flue, or the

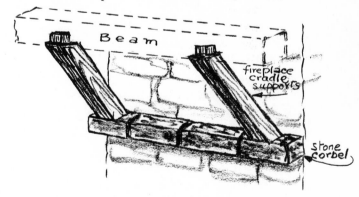

A typical hearth cradle of timber—later filled with stone. Fig. 45.

49

A very early cellar fireplace used by slaves or for household tasks such as lye-making.

flue actually added to the rear or side of the old chimney top. In the latter case an L- or T-shaped chimney top would result.

In the very oldest houses, the central chimney was built so that its top was located behind, and parallel with, the roof ridge. These chimneys were likely to be wide and shallow because all the flues were on the two sides. In contrast, with houses two rooms deep, the chimney would be more nearly square because of the kitchen flue at the rear.

Most chimneys are set in clay, at least as far as the common flue at attic level. From that point up they are more likely to be set in lime mortar. Nevertheless, the upper section would have comparatively thin walls— one brick thick or perhaps six inches of stone. This is where the fire hazard became acute, for the resinous matter from the wood fires condensed on the inside of the chimney and soaked through the clay, coating both inside and outside with tar. If the tar-soaked soot in the chimney caught fire it could quickly ignite the roof and another old house would be lost to posterity.

To discourage rainwater from running down between the chimney and the roof timbers, drip courses were formed on old chimneys. (Fig. 41.) These consisted of a single course of brick or stone set to project an inch or more beyond the chimney face. One such course would be located at the back and front of the chimney, a few inches above the roof. Another would extend across the sides of the chimney just above the ridge. These drip courses took the place of modern flashing but naturally they were not particularly effective, and the roof timbers around a chimney always need to be inspected for rot as a consequence. Incidentally, when such a chimney is flashed the drip courses should be left intact. Masons who do this kind of work seem to take a special delight in chopping them off so that they can cement the flashing into a joint higher up.

Before leaving this subject, mention should be made of the small brick flues found in the extensions and ells. Since the walls of these chimneys often are no more than nine inches thick at the lower part and one brick thick at the top they invariably

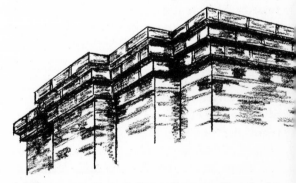

Adding an external flue often produced this pilastered (or cluster) effect on an early chimney.

leak both tar and smoke. Where they pass through an attic or roof they often lean over to strike the center of the roof ridge. Such leaning chimneys are sometimes supported by planks. In other instances, the top part of the chimney will be built on top of a roof timber, with the lower section offset so that it comes up alongside the upper part.

The great majority of these small chimneys were installed to accommodate stoves, not earlier than 1850. The patented airtight stoves in particular, so long the rage, demanded narrow flues and tall chimneys to ensure adequate draft. Often it was simplest to run a stovepipe up to a dwarf or docked chimney carried on wooden brackets just below a roof or ceiling. (Fig. 48.)

None of these chimneys should be used. In the majority of cases they are better entirely removed. But before tearing down any chimney that extends above a roof, the effect on the appearance of the house should be considered. The important thing is to make sure such chimneys are never connected to a stove or fireplace.

The Bake Oven

Every central chimney had, of necessity, to incorporate a bake oven. After about 1750 or so, the kitchen fireplaces were made somewhat smaller and the ovens built into one of the jambs so that they opened directly into the room. In such cases the oven had its own small flue, opening into the main flue at kitchen ceiling level. This flue was located just inside the oven opening, behind the small lintel.

Whether the oven was inside the fireplace or in front of it, it was provided with a sheet-iron cover that acted as a door to seal it while in use. Where there was a flue,

A typical example of a docked chimney carried on a beam. Fig. 48.

this door fitted against a lip in the masonry between the oven and the flue.

To use the bake oven, a fire was first lighted inside it. This was done by burning small wood chips in the oven opening. As these were added to, they were gradually pushed farther into the oven, the fire being kept burning briskly to create a draft inside. It took about an hour to get a good fire burning all over the oven bottom, the flames entirely filling it. At first the oven bricks would become black with soot, and when this burned off so that the bricks were once more clean, the oven was judged to be hot enough. The ashes and hot coals were raked out and in went the food—Indian pudding first, then the brown bread, the pots of beans, and finally the pies—possibly ten or a dozen of them—as they were the first to come out. With the tin door in place, the whole thing could be forgotten for several hours.

TYPICAL BAKE OVEN

Section through a bake oven and its flue.

When the oven is alongside the fireplace opening there will be a recess in the wall beneath it. This is sometimes called the ash hole, and both it and the oven are occasionally covered with a wooden door to match the paneling around the fireplace. Sometimes charring at the bottom of this door suggests that the lower opening actually was used for the hot ashes from the oven. On the other hand, many of these recesses have wooden sills and are several inches above the floor—a highly unsuitable arrangement for receiving hot coals! Logic also suggests that the oven coals could just as well be dumped in the fireplace proper —as they were with the rear-type ovens. The recess then may have been used to store the special oven fuel—hand-whittled sticks and shavings—and another fire hazard eliminated.

Bake ovens (which the uninitiated so wrongly insist on calling "Dutch" ovens) also were built into chimneys located on end walls, where the depth of the masonry was frequently not sufficient to accommodate the entire oven. In such a case the oven would be built out beyond the house wall, and supported on masonry corbels or wooden brackets let into the masonry. (Fig. 52.) In the late 19th and early 20th Centuries many of these external beehive ovens fell into disrepair and were removed. In other instances, an added wing or ell might take in the oven. In the large kitchen fireplaces, other recesses might be provided in the masonry for utensils, fire-lighting equipment, and so on.

In Pennsylvania many of the old bake ovens are set in the back or side of the large kitchen fireplace, and are fitted with an

52

In the earliest central chimney houses, the bake oven was located in the back wall of the kitchen fireplace as seen here. (*Courtesy Mrs. Arthur Warwick*)

Later houses had the bake oven alongside the fireplace with an "ashpit."

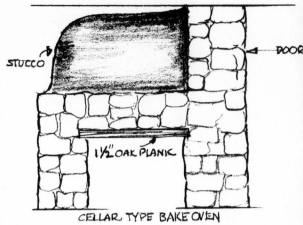

CELLAR TYPE BAKE OVEN

Cellar bake oven in early Pennsylvania stone house.

A brick beehive oven projecting from a gable wall. Fig. 52.

iron door that incorporates a latch. Otherwise their construction is the same as elsewhere, with stone bases and brick arches and domes.

Smoke Chambers

In some of the later attics will be found a boxlike structure attached to the chimney, a glistening black inside, and probably showing signs of charring. This is a smoke chamber or smoke oven used for curing meats. Smoke was generated by corn cobs or hickory bark smoldering in a metal pot on the chamber floor. The smoke would rise to the top, where the meats hung on hooks, and pass into the chimney through a hole in the stack.

Sometimes the smoke chamber floor may be of bare wood or covered with sheet iron. Doors might be similarly protected, but in very many instances the inside of the chamber would be lath and plaster. Smoke chambers of brick or of wood are also found alongside the chimney in the kitchen, on the stair landing, or even in the cellar. If these ovens are restored, the hole into the chimney should be sealed, but any wooden structure attached to the chimney is a fire hazard and is best eliminated.

Three early fireplaces in Pennsylvania stone houses.

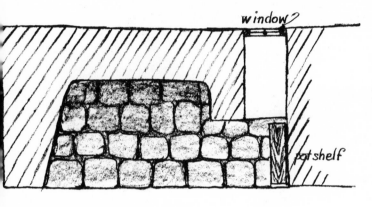

Fine panelling over a Pennsylvania Dutch living room fireplace of stuccoed stone. (*Courtesy Mrs. Edward L. Webster*)

A lath-and-plaster smoke chamber attached to an earlier chimney. Note door removed, exposing charred lathing.

Chapter IV

The Shapes of Houses

DURING the first one hundred and fifty years of British colonial occupation of these shores, a great many primitive houses were constructed in Virginia Colony and New England. After a period of thatched roofs and mud-daubed walls, the colonists settled down to serious building. Even from the first some were considerably more ambitious than others, and this has led to some confusion in the dating of old houses and the tracing of their development. Logic here does not seem to work. It is now well known that many of the more elaborate houses—those with two or more rooms on the ground floor—were not necessarily built *after* the smaller, simpler ones; nor were all the larger houses originally small ones. The opposite was a natural conclusion not justified by later known facts. The dating of houses, as we shall see presently, is an extremely complicated subject, and crudity of plan or construction does not alone spell antiquity.

In both North and South, the simplest of the primitive houses consisted of a single room with a loft for sleeping over it. Even in such a house there had to be a fireplace for cooking and heating. In New England this one-room plan was developed into a two-room style of house known colloquially, in the North, as a "saltbox" (a term not countenanced by architects, with some reason!) and in the South as a "catslide" house.

It is a common error to assume that this type of leanto house was a Colonial invention. There are many small houses of this shape and construction in England, both in masonry and in wood. And there would have been many more if their owners had stopped adding outshots at that point. In any event, this type of house proved so useful and convenient in the eyes of the Colonists that many houses were built in the leanto style, with the leanto an integral part of the original plan.

This brings us naturally to a detailed consideration of these and other well-known styles of Colonial houses. First let us take a look at the early New England types that have one thing in common—a centrally-placed chimney. These are: (1) the leanto, (2) the one and one half to two and a half story Early American, and (3) Cape-Cod.

The Leanto House

All central-chimney houses have essentially the same floor plan. The differences, insofar as the main floor is concerned, are

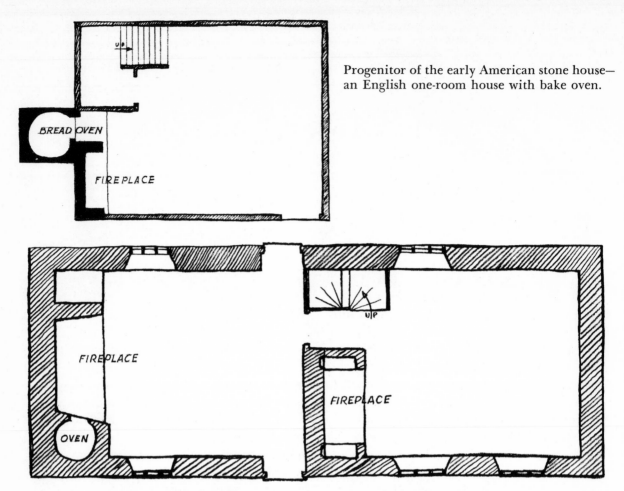

Progenitor of the early American stone house—
an English one-room house with bake oven.

A 16th-Century English stone house with gable fireplace and bake oven.

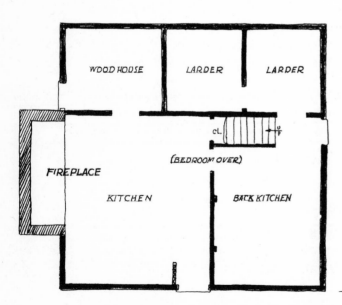

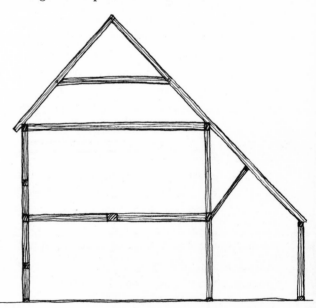

How the English two-room plan was developed
into the earliest "saltbox."

The framing of a 16th-Century "saltbox."

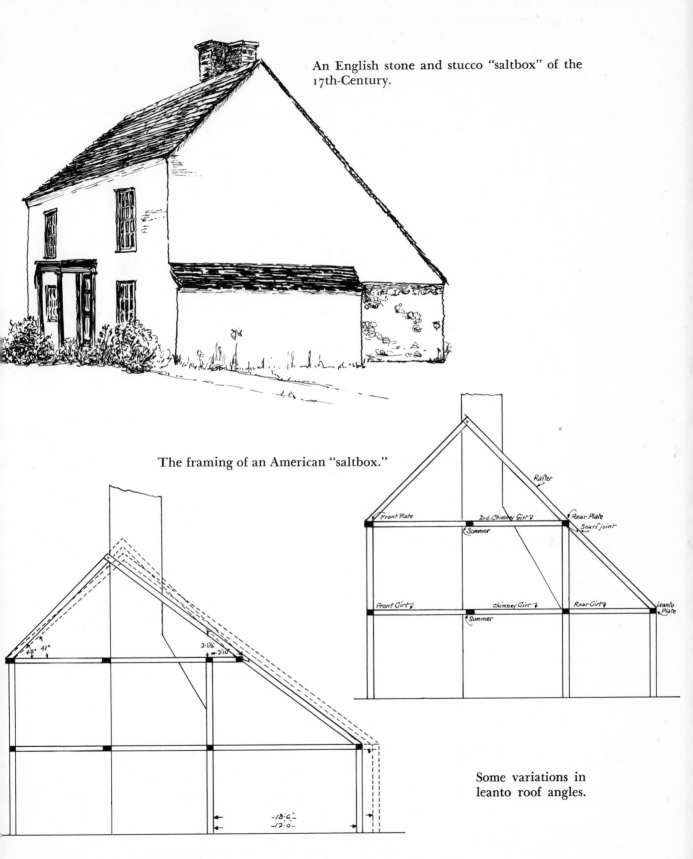

An English stone and stucco "saltbox" of the 17th-Century.

The framing of an American "saltbox."

Some variations in leanto roof angles.

59

largely governed by the depth of the rear rooms. In the case of the leanto house, the important thing was to get the kitchen behind the chimney, releasing the keeping-room for other things. Since the new kitchen did not need to be very deep—say nine to twelve feet—the rear leanto could be added without breaking the rear roof line very much. In other words, the new leanto rafters could be joined to those of the original roof. The continuous roof solved the problem of making a weather-tight joint between the two.

INTERIOR SPACE IN "SALTBOXES"

The floor plans of the northern leanto houses, in their original state, vary very little. With a large central chimney, having fireplaces on two sides and the back, there is only one possible arrangement of the ground floor.

The front door opens into a small entry that occupies the full width of the chimney. This entry is often no more than eight feet wide and six feet deep. Doors from this open into one room on each side of the chimney—the keeping room and the parlor. To get to the rear rooms it is necessary to pass through one of these. At the rear of the chimney will be the large kitchen in the leanto section of the house. This compara-tively shallow leanto gives the house two more rooms in addition to the kitchen with its big fireplace—a buttery on the north, or colder side, and a small bedroom or "born-ing room" at the warmer gable. The origin of the term "borning room" must be ob-vious; being near the main fireplace it would always be warm and close to the supply of hot water. The kitchen is nor-mally as long as the chimney plus the width of two doors—fifteen to seventeen feet or over.

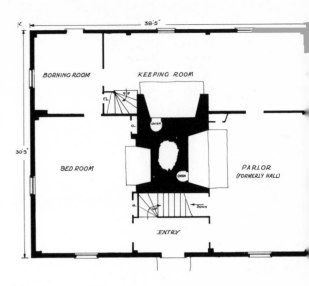

First and second floor plans of the Ogden House shown on Page 35, Fig. 23.

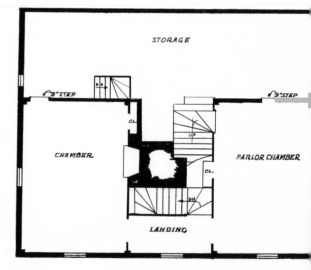

In the majority of cases a rear stair to the upper floor (and perhaps to the cellar) goes up out of one end of the kitchen. Access to the second floor from the front of the house is by a stair from the front porch or entry. The arrangement of these stairs and their proportions depends upon the depth of the porch. That, in turn, is governed by the location of the chimney. The nearer the chimney is to the front wall of the house, the narrower the stair, and the steeper. With an entry 8 feet deep, the stair can be three and one-half to four feet wide, and one or more steps can project into the porch and into the upstairs landing. This often provides sufficient length of stair run to allow for reasonably low steps, and the use of platforms at the turns in place of "pie steps"—winders. But unless the chimney is at least ten feet wide, a really comfortable run of stairs is impossible. In so many of these houses the depth of the entry is barely sufficient to allow for a three-foot front door swinging wide open, and the stair may be barely two-feet, six-inches wide, with steps eight or nine inches high. In some instances the door has to be double—i.e. made in two separate panels.

In most leanto houses the second floor has a small landing over the porch. This gives access to a bedroom on either side. In turn, each of the bedrooms is connected by a doorway to the space running across the back of the house under the leanto roof. Quite often you will find that the attic floor is boarded over, and access to it afforded by a ladder, or very steep stair, alongside the chimney. In some "saltboxes" there is a fireplace in one or both bedrooms —called the parlor chamber and the hall chamber respectively.

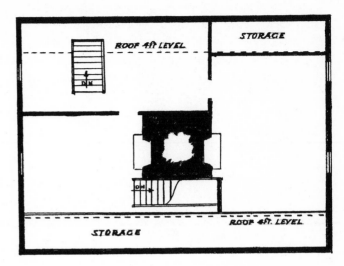

First and second floor plans of one and one-half story Early American.

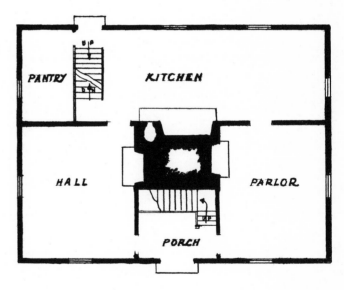

Two ideas for utilizing the usually cramped space in a "saltbox" second floor area. A stair may be at one end, a tiny bathroom at the other. (*Courtesy of Mr. & Mrs. Reinhold Gieseler and Mr. & Mrs. Fred Baker*)

Typical built-in corner cupboard in an 18th-Century "salt-box" farm house (door missing). (*Courtesy of Miss Janie Pierce*)

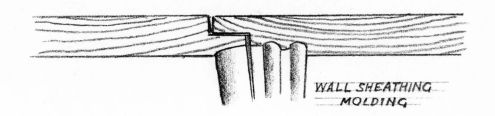

A great many early leantos owe much of their interior attraction to the fact that one or more rooms are paneled or panel-sheathed, and may even have built-in corner cupboards. In many instances the sheathing of the original keeping room was done after the new leanto fireplace had been built and the old one cut down in size.

THE LEANTO ROOF

In acquiring a "saltbox" type of house it is always interesting to know whether or not the leanto was originally part of the house or a later addition. This, unfortunately, is not of much help in determining the age of the house.

In order to ascertain the original construction it is necessary to examine the rear roof timbers. If the rafters extend in one piece from the ridge to the rear, first-floor eaves, the house was almost certainly built as a "saltbox." If the leanto rafters are pieced into the main roof rafters at the second floor plate, it may possibly be a later addition, but the evidence is by no means conclusive. At a later period when large timbers were not so readily available, it would be logical to make these rear roofs with shorter rafters scarved together.

Much commoner is this use of rear rafters in two sections—the upper section reaching only down to the top plate. These sections would be fastened into the top of the plate with a notched or step joint, the lower lengths being scarved into the upper rafter feet. (Fig. 64.) This gives a continuous upper surface to the rafter, level with the outer corner of the plate.

An arrangement of this kind might suggest the later addition of the leanto, but in few instances would the upper length extend far enough beyond the plate to form a scarf joint. Therefore, unless the original roof had a deep overhang, the two sections of rafter must have been installed at the same time and the house designed as a "saltbox." In other words, where the two lengths of rafter are connected by a scarf joint, notched to the plate, the inference is that the leanto was part of the original structure. In a purlin roof particularly, it is always advisable to check the rafters for joints between the plate and the ridge. Sometimes the rafters were lengthened by adding a section to the upper end. In cases where the lower rafters are fastened to the top plate *alongside* the roof rafters, it is almost certain that the leanto was a later addition.

Another interesting and revealing roof detail to watch for is the method of raising the rafters above the second-story plate. This was sometimes done to make possible a deeper and higher ceilinged leanto room on the ground floor. Where this was planned originally, the two halves of the main roof almost certainly would be of the same pitch. If it were done later, the rear roof would slope at a lesser angle than the front slope, moving the ridge line forward. Where the rear roof was originally planned for a leanto, the rafters may be supported

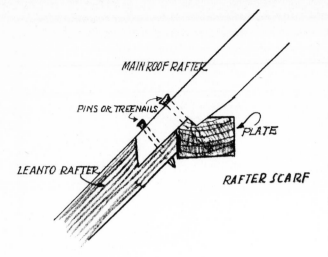

Leanto rafter scarf joint in 18th-Century "saltbox." Fig. 64.

on rearward extensions of the second girts. The two halves of the roof would then have the same pitch.

Where the individual girts support the rafters, extra girts take the place of the top floor ceiling joists. This ordinarily happens when the roof is formed of principal rafters, and the girts form the lower members of the roof trusses. For example, if there were six pairs of principal rafters there would be six girts (really oversized rafters) halved over the rear plate. These would be framed into the six leanto rafters.

More common than this, apparently, was the practice of extending the four regular girts and supporting another plate on their ends. This plate would then carry the common rafters for both upper and lower roofs. This plate might be two, or even three, feet behind the rear plate of the main house.

In cases where the roof raising was performed at a later period, the rafters may be supported on blocks laid on top of the original plate. But again this is not indisputable evidence that the original house was not a "saltbox." Signs must also be sought of raising of the leanto roof and rear

wall. A variation of this blocking is found in houses where a second plate is mounted above the original one, and really acts as a purlin for the rear roof rafters.

From all of this it must be evident that dating leanto houses from the roof structure is not a simple matter. And the fact still remains that a "saltbox" with an added leanto may, or may not, be older than a house designed and built with a leanto originally.

While the leanto added rooms to the ground floor it provided little usable space upstairs. To secure an equal amount of

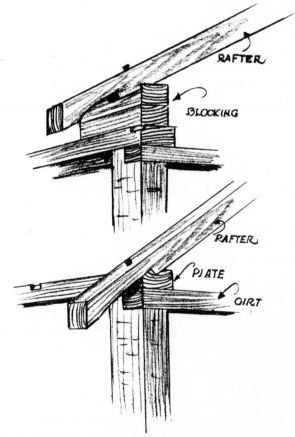

How rear rafters were "blocked" to flatten angle of leanto roof.

64

space on the second floor, a full two-story addition was called for—an expensive business because an entirely new roof would have to be provided. Nevertheless, sometimes the leanto house was later remodeled into a full two-story house two rooms deep. To get full-sized bedchambers at the rear it was necessary to start from the leanto ceiling up. Where this has been done, the second floor posts will be found framed into the first floor plate. In other instances a better job will have been done by starting fresh from the foundations.

Houses originally two rooms deep to which a leanto has been added are not true "saltboxes," and few, if any, were ever built in that form in the 18th Century. In the majority of such houses there will be a definite "break" in the line of the rear roof. Such a break in any "saltbox" roof usually indicates a later leanto addition.

Early American (Center-Chimney)

The central-chimney Early American is one of the commonest surviving types of antique house. It varies considerably in size and accommodations, and in the locations of added extensions. You will find these houses in one, one and a half, two, and two and a half story heights, with or without an overhang.

In the one and one-half-story Early American the gabled roof comes down to within two to four feet of the upper-floor level. Ordinarily there are no windows in the upper half-story, either front or rear. All other windows for that floor are in the gables. These houses are always two rooms deep so that the roof is high in proportion to the façade. On the first floor there is a central door in line with the chimney, and one or two windows on either side of it.

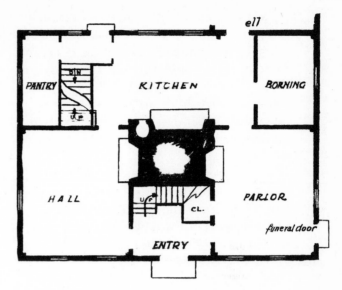

Floor plan for two-story Early American.

One of the downstairs front rooms is the parlor and this is provided with a funeral door, since it is somewhat awkward maneuvering a casket through the narrow entry to the front door. At the rear of the chimney the space is usually divided into three rooms in the same manner as the "saltbox," the center one having a kitchen fireplace.

Because of the low sweep of the roof, which limits the headroom upstairs near the front wall, it is impossible to have a second-floor landing in the usual position. Some of the old-time builders overcame this by starting the stair against the chimney wall and turning it back at right angles to go over a shoulder of the chimney. This "shoulder" was formed by keeping the flue from the parlor fireplace as low as possible, and running it at a flat angle into the main stack. The main run of the stair is then up toward the rear of the house. This introduces a passage or hallway from the stack to the back wall of the house, giving access to two rooms on each side.

65

An alternative to this stair arrangement is found in some houses that have a Y-shaped stair against the face of the chimney, with an upper landing from front to rear along one side of the stack. This allows for a fair-sized chamber and a smaller one at one gable, the opposite chamber being about four feet less in width on account of the passageway.

The principal drawback of this type of house is that the low ceiling at the front and rear walls limits the use of the floor space in these areas. That is why the rear rooms

One and one-half story Early American with "eyebrow" windows.

are usually quite narrow, and the front rooms have a slice taken off them to form storage rooms or walk-in closets. The result is that there are only two sizable bedrooms upstairs in most one and a half story Early Americans. In cases where the up-

stairs walls are four feet or so high, there may be a rear window to light the upper hallway or even low windows front and rear. If the walls are lower there will perhaps be a series of "eyebrow" or "lie-on-your-stomach" windows that have been inserted under the eaves.

The full two-story house of course suffers none of these disadvantages. The stair, which may have two sets of winders if the ceilings are low and the chimney narrow, is at least compact. Above the entry is a landing giving access to the bedrooms on either side. To get to the rear rooms it is often necessary to go through the front ones. More often than not, however, there will be a rear stair leading to the second-floor back rooms. This stair itself naturally introduces complications because it takes up space on the second floor. Unless it was carefully planned it will waste a lot of space on passageways to the two, or three, rear rooms. This is the reason why many of these houses were finished with only one rear bedroom, leaving a great deal of space for storage. On the other hand, the total useful floor space is much greater with the higher second-floor ceilings and the two-story house does have the important advantage of providing windows in front and rear walls upstairs, as well as in the gables. A much lighter and airier house results.

In both the one and a half and two-story Early American houses this problem of access and stair placement is relieved when there is a wing on the house, as we shall see later. The only other important difference between the accommodations in these two houses is the presence of a useful attic in the two-story unit—accessible via the rear stair.

The Cape Cod Style House

In the late 17th Century and early 18th Century there was developed in the Massachusetts Bay Colony a two-room-deep, central-chimney type of single-story house that came to be known as the Cape Cod style. The sheer simplicity of its design, its compactness, and its eminent suitability to the climate of the wind-swept Cape ensured it of a popularity that continues to this day.

The original Cape Cod house had two basic characteristics—a four-square plan, and a sweeping, moderately high-pitched roof that came down to the first-floor ceiling height. A one-story house, it still had stairs and limited accommodations within the roof. Strangely enough, some of the earliest of these houses were given a gambrel roof —either originally or later—in order to afford more space upstairs without increasing the main floor area. Whether or not they can, with this type of roof, continue to be classed as Cape Cod houses is open to debate. Since they do, in effect, become story-and-a-half houses, we are inclined to think they forfeit that right.

Another variation of the full Cape Cod is the half-house, quite common in that area. This has the appearance of the full Cape Cod house with one end cut off at the chimney. No doubt most of them were built with the idea of some day adding the extension to give them the full Cape Cod plan. All the upstairs windows are in the gables of the true Cape Cod and there are no dormers. Ordinarily, the Cape Cod house was built on symmetrical lines. The front entrance occupied the center of the façade, flanked by a pair of windows, and the chimney was centered. On the other hand, there

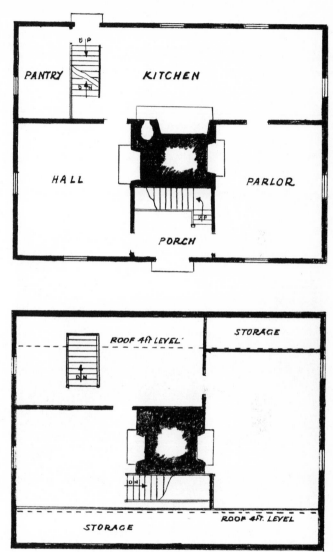

A typical "Cape Cod" house floor plan.
Fig. 68.

67

are quite a few surviving examples of asymmetrical houses with the sweeping Cape Cod-style roof but somewhat modified floor plan.

All the original Cape Cod houses were built of wood, often, it is said, by ship's carpenters at whose doors the bowed or "rainbow" roof is laid. Unluckily for that theory, houses with bowed roofs are also found in East Anglia. There are several, very old houses with their roofs curved upwards from eaves to ridge on Cape Cod, Nantucket, and Martha's Vineyard, but it is questionable whether they gain anything by that innovation.

An original Connecticut "Cape Cod"—about 1780.

In plan, the Cape Cod house normally had no more than the usual entry, hall and parlor, with a long kitchen and pantry behind them. A feature of many of these houses is the extensive use of paneling. Where the second floor was used, the stair would probably be located between the kitchen and the pantry. This would lead up to a long rear storage room behind the chimney. At the stair end of the upper floor would be a small bedroom, and at the other gable a larger bedroom the full depth of the house at standing height. In front of the chimney might be a narrow stair up to the storage loft under the ridge. This stair would lead from the small bedchamber. Such a plan is illustrated (Fig. 68). Like the rest of the central-chimney houses, the Cape Cod house invariably acquired an ell, or sometimes a one-story extension or wing.

Outshots and Attachments

Since practically all of these Early American houses do have dependencies and attachments of one sort or another, it may be helpful to examine some of the commoner arrangements at this point. The most usual, and undoubtedly the most convenient, method of enlarging these houses was to add a rear ell. This could be done without spoiling any of the rear roof or cutting off too much light. In this connection it is an interesting fact that in many cases the ells were built before the main house was erected. Sometimes it seems as though the ell was used as a home while the main structure was being built on to it. Some of these ells also appear to have been moved from another site and attached to a newer house. These are possibilities to be considered in studying the history of any old house.

The principal purpose for adding an ell to an Early American-style house in the North was to provide extra ground-floor space and greater convenience by moving the kitchen out of the house proper. Many such ells therefore have a substantial chimney and kitchen fireplace of their own. In

There's always something very appealing about a gambrel-roofed house.

some instances one or more fireplaces would be added to the same ell chimney to serve additional rooms beyond the kitchen. In the colder sections of the country, the ell might continue on indefinitely, forming a sheltered passageway to woodshed, wagon shed, the well, etc. and ending only at the privy!

Such an ell might be wide enough to extend from one gable more than half the length of the rear wall. This would eliminate the old kitchen window, and the borning room partition might have to be removed to let in light from the gable window. Most of the ells, however, seem to have been kept narrow enough to leave the original kitchen window, or windows, unobstructed.

Wings attached to the gables of Early American houses had to be more carefully planned than the ells if they were not to spoil the looks of the house. The roof ridge must needs run parallel with the house ridge, and the whole structure be neither too skimpy nor too overpowering. In this, even the early carpenters seem to have been eminently successful.

As a rule, the wing is set back from the front of the house. Its back wall may be in line with that of the house or slightly to the rear of it. Sometimes the front of the single-story wing will have its roof extended to form a porch. In practically every instance the wing will have a fireplace and chimney at its gable. This wing often contains a kitchen—perhaps only a "summer kitchen," or one used only for the more messy or unpleasant household chores such as rendering lard, dyeing, or candlemaking. Such a wing usually has its external entrance.

69

Peaked-roof extensions adapted to gambrels.
(*Courtesy Mr. George C. Lyon*)

One way of adapting a "Cape Cod" to a growing family.
(*Courtesy Mr. & Mrs. Fred Jewell*)

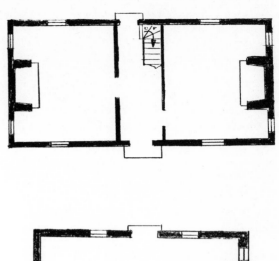

One advantage of a wing was that it sometimes provided the opportunity of moving the rear stairs of the house to a less obtrusive position. The stair could then rise out of the new kitchen, giving access to the roof space (a suitable sleeping space for a servant) and, by means of a door in the old gable, to the second floor of the house.

Two-story wings are quite common on houses of two stories and over. Usually the upper story is connected by a door directly into the house. In some cases, the upper floor of the wing then is used to provide extra bedchambers and may not be connected by a stair with its own main floor.

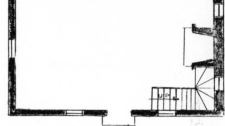

Houses of the Virginia Colony

Like their contemporaries in New England, the Virginia colonists from the begin-

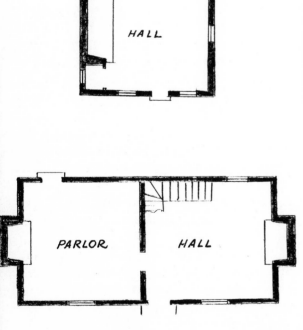

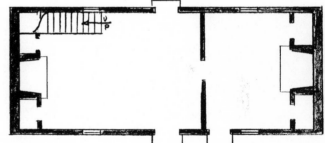

Floor plans of smaller southern Colonial houses.

ning based the design and construction of their houses on those they had known in England. The first of these houses were primitive structures that by 1615 had developed into half-timbered two-story dwellings. Soon thereafter, the exposed frames were covered with weatherboards. Brickyards

A Virginia chimney—they are not always built away from the gable.

had been established by this time and the construction of the larger all-brick houses and mansions already begun. These substantial houses, which belonged to the more prosperous members of the community, were from the beginning outnumbered by simple, braced-frame houses of wood. But by 1700, the smaller houses of brick were being built in increasing numbers. As in the case of New England, early houses of the Virginia Colony show a distinct line of development from the one-room-plan cottage to the two-room central-hall-plan with leantos. But here again size and complexity are no guide to chronology. From the end of the 17th Century even the smallest houses were often built of brick and the wooden ones had elaborate chimneys. These chimneys were incorporated in the gable walls, sometimes projecting into the room, sometimes extending outward from the gable. In a great many instances a house had both types, in which case the larger chimney, incorporating a kitchen-type fireplace, would be outside the gable. To put such a massive affair inside the house would obviously have necessitated a larger room and much waste space. Continuing this larger chimney upward, level with the back of the fireplace, while reducing it in size, resulted in the upper, smaller section being spaced a few inches away from the gable. This was not done as a fire precaution, as is so often stated, otherwise *both* chimneys would have been treated in the same fashion.

The frames in these brick houses consisted solely of horizontal timbers supported on corbels or in recesses in the masonry; there were no vertical timbers except for the partitions. In the wooden houses, when there were end chimneys and complete, or

72

Virginia gambrels are usually of the English type—narrow and steep.

partial masonry gables, the braced frame as known in New England had to be modified. The central chimney girts became the entry girts, and the end girts turned into chimney girts. Beyond this, the frame may have been extended either to the outside or inside face of the gable. But there would be no transverse frame member at this point. In some instances the roof gable would be entirely of wood, set on the masonry walls which would be topped by a plate.

These houses were but one room deep, and whether made of brick or wood, the natural line of development was the addition of a rear leanto, thus forming a "cat-slide" house. When this rear section was built a full two stories, the chimneys were centered in the gables, and so formed an Early-Georgian style house.

Many of the one-room-deep houses with a central hall and end chimneys were built one story high. Dormers were then added to the steep roofs to increase the usable space upstairs. This was the case with both frame and brick houses. All of these types are in existence today.

Few of the early houses had cellars, and brick floors were popular. In the smallest houses a bake oven was built into the side of the fireplace, but most of the two-room plans or larger houses had no such structure. The baking was done in ovens built outside and separate from the house. Whether the early house is of brick or wood its roof will be of the ridge type, though gambrels became popular soon after 1700. At about the same time it became common practice to increase accommodations by adding a leanto at the rear of the house, producing the "catslide" equivalent of the New England "saltbox." In the later and better houses the lower floors were raised a foot or so from the ground as a means of reducing dampness and enabling wooden floors to be used.

All of the wooden houses with the exception of the earlier 17th-Century half-timbered dwellings were of the braced-frame type covered with clapboards and roofed with shingles. Many were of one or two stories high, but the favored type was the one and a half story, with dormers either original or as later additions.

The Georgian House

By 1720, the two-story house, two rooms deep, was common. The general prosperity was increasing, bringing with it a growing demand for better and more important-looking houses. During the next thirty years, existing houses were made more attractive by external additions that reflected the style of the larger houses and mansions. The simple doorways were dressed up with pediments and pilasters, the plain windows ornamented with molded architraves. The façades were given an air of importance and solidity by replacing corner boards with pilasters and quoins; the roofs finished off with box cornices trimmed with moldings and supported by dentils. Inside, the doors and windows of these houses were made elegant with applied moldings, and the rooms finished with picture moldings and cornice moldings.

All of this heralded the adoption of the Early Georgian style of architecture for houses of modest size. Meanwhile bricks were becoming more plentiful, and therefore cheaper, making it possible to build smaller chimneys at less cost than the old masonry piles featured in early New England houses. Those who built new houses at this time could therefore well afford to adopt the new style, and have two chimneys instead of one. They did, however, adhere to the practice of keeping the chimneys entirely within the house by building them into the longitudinal walls. The chimneys of the northern Early Georgian houses therefore usually center on the ridge at a distance of several feet in from the gables. Each chimney provided two fireplaces back to back on the main floor, and could incorporate two more on the second floor if desired.

This radical change in chimney location made possible a much more flexible floor plan. With a central hall, circulation—of air as well as people—was considerably improved, and a much better stair arrangement could be adopted. This stair now gave access to each second-floor room.

In many of these Early Georgian houses, the kitchen was relegated to an ell, leaving one of the rear rooms usable as a dining room. From about 1750 on, until after the

A simple but delightful brick Georgian, painted yellow. The Rankin
House, Glastonbury, Conn. (*Courtesy of Mr. & Mrs. Thomas F. Theurkauf*)

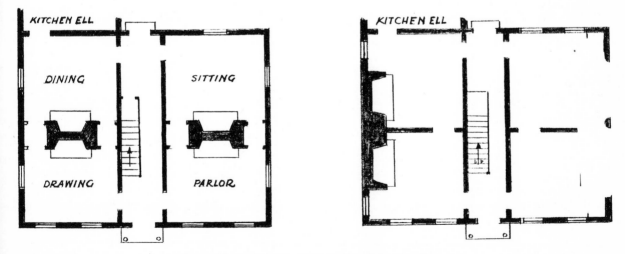

Some Georgian houses had gable fireplaces.
Others were built into the longitudinal walls.

An attractive Georgian farmhouse of the later 18th Century.

Revolution, a great many fully developed Georgian houses were built. These had chimneys in the gable walls, and the former high-ridged roofs gave way to low and inconspicuous ones, sometimes entirely hidden by a balustrade and crowned by a captain's walk (or widow's walk if you prefer the more somber designation!).

In some of these houses, the chimneys for each pair of end rooms would merge and appear as a single stack at each end of the ridge. In the larger houses, four separate stacks would be carried up to adorn a hipped roof.

While more and more of these houses were built of brick, even in New England, still more were of wood that simulated stone or brick. In the later Georgians, larger windows with bigger panes balanced one another in a symmetrical façade. Doorways were framed with sidelights and pillared porticoes, and a Palladian window above it replaced the single flat-topped window after 1750 or so. After 1790, square-topped triple

76

A square plan-hipped roof Georgian house with wooden quoins and Palladian window.

windows may have been used instead. Windows and doors alike were pedimented. Then, to make the houses even more imposing, they were mounted on a high foundation reached by broad masonry steps.

One of the finest examples we know of American Georgian architecture is the Wentworth-Gardner house at Portsmouth, N.H. This stately house, which was built in 1760, incorporates all the best features of the later style, including a lovely fifteen-panel door enframed by fluted Corinthian pilasters and surmounted by an exquisite

A small Pennsylvania stone farmhouse, built in two sections and stuccoed. A pent roof appears to have been removed. (*Courtesy Mr. & Mrs. John Knecht*)

scrolled pediment in the center of which is a gilt pineapple, ancient symbol of hospitality.

The whole façade, with its nine tall windows—the lower ones have triangular pediments—is formed of wooden blocks simulating vee-jointed stone, similar to those of Mount Vernon. The corners, likewise, have massive quoins also of wood. The hipped roof with its two tall chimneys has a cluster of three dormers, the two outside ones with triangular pediments and the center one arched.

In Pennsylvania, particularly in the

Philadelphia area, the Early Georgian houses were mostly built of brick or stone. The earlier stone houses were of rough, undressed stone, sometimes hidden beneath a coat of stucco. Later on, dressed stone was used, adding to the feel of formality. In parts of Maryland and Delaware, decorative brick walls became the fashion by mid-century. Gables and façades were enlivened with patterns in the glazed ends of over-burned bricks.

In both early and late Georgian houses a great deal of attention was paid to detail. Formality was the keynote, inside and out. Paint in an extensive variety of colors, rather than white, replaced the naked pine interiors. Ornamental corner cupboards were built in, and Early Georgian fireplace walls were encased in panels. In the later years the panelled walls were replaced by dadoes with a papered wall above them.

Both to provide extra interior space, and to give a more imposing appearance to the Georgian houses, dormers were sometimes added. In the Early Georgians with their gabled roofs these dormers were usually square with a peaked roof ("dog-house" dormers, as they were called in the South). In later designs the dormer windows were

A particularly fine Delaware Georgian in brick. The Read House, Newcastle, Delaware. (*Courtesy New York Historical Society*)

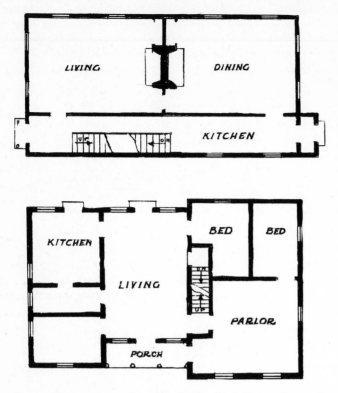

Two contrasting Greek Revival floor plans of the early 19th Century. Fig. 80.

surmounted by a complete pediment, either triangular or arched. In the larger houses with four dormers, two might be arched and two triangular.

The Greek Revival

The interest in buildings of classic style gained momentum after the Revolution. By 1820 it had culminated in an entirely new type of smaller house in what we call the Greek Revival style. In these houses design was no longer simply a matter of proportion and decoration. Even the floor plan was changed and variable, and the ideal exterior was that of a Greek temple complete with columns and architraves, friezes and cornices—the complete entablature decorated with running frets, anthemions, acanthus leaves and paterae.

The time, incidentally, was ripe for such a change. Not only were the former colonists anxious to develop a style of architecture that was not borrowed from the mother country, but the Georgian architecture had lost much of its virility. A change of some sort was needed and the architects and builders of the new Republic seized upon the ancient classic designs of that other early Republic, Greece.

Within a few decades the classical concept had been run into the ground, particularly by the builders of small houses who changed proportions and mixed styles to suit their own uneducated ideas. Meanwhile, however, some charming small houses in the Greek Revival style had been built, and many remain to grace the American landscape to this day.

The two major types of Greek Revival houses of small size were developed. In one, the gable became the main front of the house. (Fig. 82.) This was the simplest way of crowning the façade with a classic pediment. Since the gable, for the same reason, could be only a little more than one room wide, the main entrance had to be to one side of the façade. The floor plan then consisted of two rooms with a wide hall alongside them, running from front to back. In this hall were located the stairs, and behind the stairs was the kitchen—long and narrow. (Fig. 80.)

With the other type of floor plan, a pedimented gable again dominated the façade but did not incorporate the main entrance. Set slightly back from this front line was a side extension of the house whose principal feature was a recessed porch. This porch was spanned by an architrave supported, usually, by two columns, with a pilaster at each end.

Greek Revival features of a New England farmhouse—pedimented gable, corner pilasters and elongated gable window.

From the center of this porch, the main doorway opened into a living room that extended the depth of the house. Sometimes there was another recessed porch at the back, or even on the side. A second door opened from the end into the parlor in the gabled portion. Two other small rooms behind the parlor, a dining room and kitchen on the other side of the living room, and sometimes another small room at the front completed the first-floor plan. Between the living room and the parlor were the stairs to the second floor and the cellar. (Fig. 80.)

These floor plans seem infinitely variable, and the exteriors differed just as widely. Houses of other types were often altered to give them a classical air, and usually were spoiled in the process. Some of the characteristic features of the Greek Revival house

not already mentioned were massive pilasters and architrave framing the front door; tall windows with carved trim; "eyebrow" windows with decorative gratings; and heavy overhanging eaves. Two-story pilasters—usually four in number—divided the windows and doors of the gable façade; eaves were supported on decorative friezes; the doors had deeply recessed panels, and square porticos guarded the main entrance.

Somewhere between 1800 and 1840 there were built a great many small one and a half story houses on the Early American, central-chimney plan, with modified classical features. (Fig. 83.) These might be called "farm-house" Greek Revivals. They had the plain corner pilasters and flat, undecorated architraves around doors and windows; they had overhanging eaves and a broad, plain frieze into which was let a

A smaller northern Greek revival with gable as the main front. Fig. 82.

A common feature of one and one-half story houses remodeled with Greek Revival features was the earlier series of "eyebrow" windows. Fig. 83.

A small stone Pennsylvania farmhouse carefully restored, with pent roof. (*Courtesy of Mrs. Edward L. Webster*)

series of "eyebrow" windows, innocent of any grating. These windows were hinged with butts at the top and swung inward for ventilation almost at floor level. Occasionally you will find a two and one-half-story house on the same pattern, with eyebrow windows not only front and back but also in the gables!

Chapter V

Guides to Antiquity

AT THIS particular period in history, very few houses come on the market that are more than two hundred and twenty-five years old, thanks to the historical societies and individuals interested in preserving the really ancient specimens. On the other hand, it occasionally happens that an unspoiled Colonial of early vintage may escape the eye of the antiquarian, or the local historical society may be unable to raise the necessary funds to acquire it. Apart from these rare opportunities of salvaging a worthwhile relic of another age, most antique houses acquired for restoration date from the later 18th to the middle 19th centuries. In other words, they may be anywhere from one hundred to two hundred years old.

But any house that has survived even one century is almost certain to have undergone major surgery more than once. The simpler the original house, the more likely it is to have been the victim of changing fashions, just as many an old Chippendale chair was consigned to the attic when carved oak became the hallmark of gentility. Beautiful door latches, and even the raised-panel doors themselves were eagerly traded for "modern" ones in the mid-19th Century. The old windows were replaced with large-paned sashes and even the frames thrown out so that weight-balanced sashes could be installed. Leantos and shed dormers were added, and massive chimneys were replaced with piddling single flues.

Fireplaces were bricked up, holes cut in hearthstones and tiny chimneys substituted when a stove in every room became the latest thing in heating. Interiors were remodelled with fancy moldings and doorways replaced with arches—the list is endless, and each change dictated by whim or fashion long ago today adds to the difficulty of deciding what was original in the old house, and how far to go in restoration. Undoubtedly the soundest guide is the date or period in which the house was built; and the type of house will usually determine the style of exterior finish.

The date is therefore the first thing to ascertain. Estimation of the type and layout of the house unfortunately does not throw much light on its age. If you can dig up an old will or a deed, or a bill for materials, or even correspondence in which there is reference to the property and some of its identifying features you will be unusually fortunate. Family records are always the best means of verifying the age of a house—and the scarcest. But simple refer-

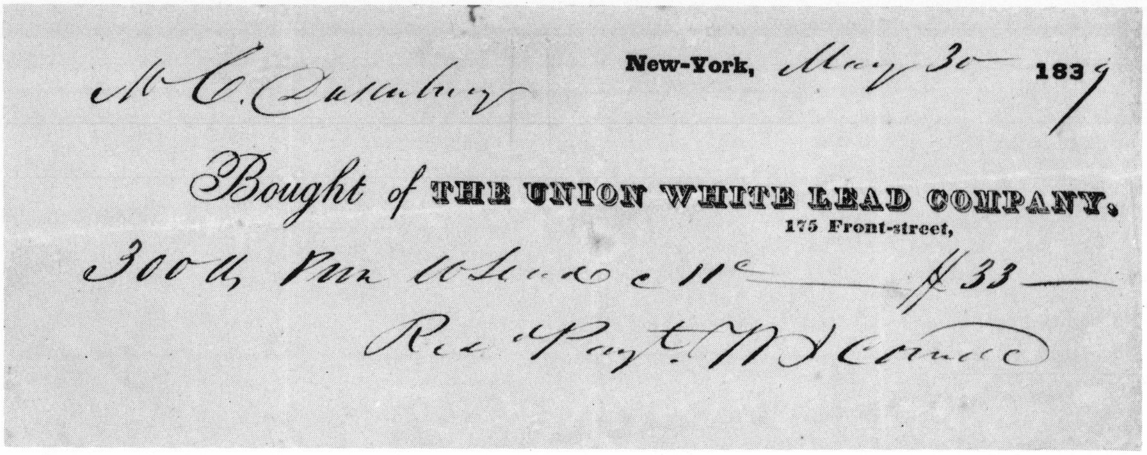

M. C. Dusenbury

New-York, *May 30* 183*9*

Bought of **THE UNION WHITE LEAD COMPANY,**
175 Front-street,

300 tt, Pure White Lead @ 11¢ — $33 —

Rec'd Pay't. W. A. Conner

M

A GENERAL ASSORTMENT OF
Scotch Hollow-Ware

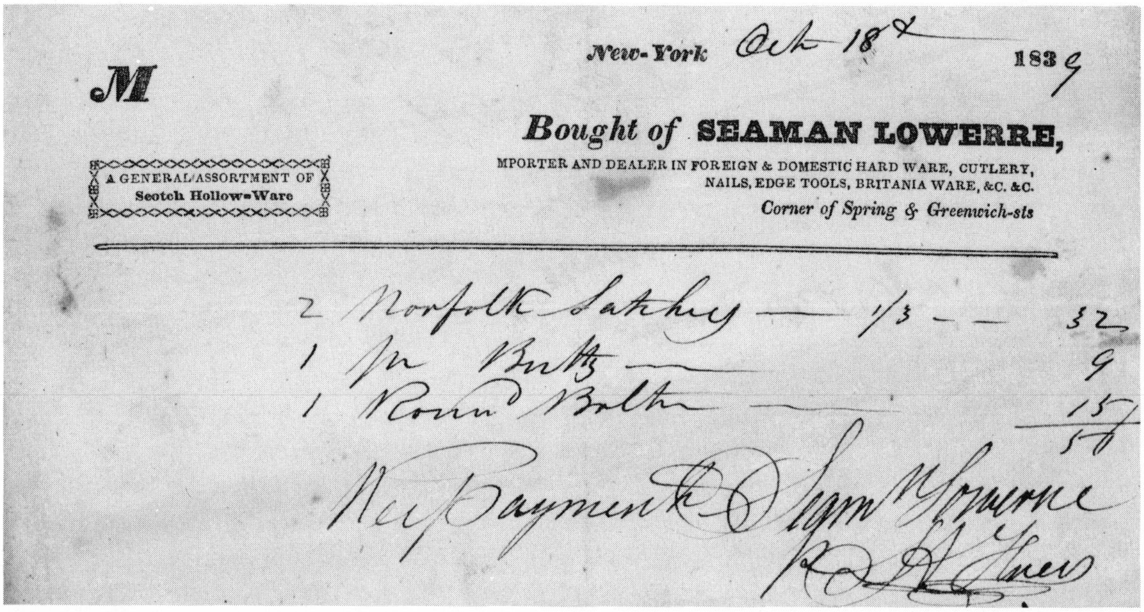

New-York Oct 18 183*9*

Bought of SEAMAN LOWERRE,
IMPORTER AND DEALER IN FOREIGN & DOMESTIC HARD WARE, CUTLERY,
NAILS, EDGE TOOLS, BRITANIA WARE, &C. &C.

Corner of Spring & Greenwich-sts

2 Norfolk Latches	1/3	— —	32
1 pr Butts			9
1 Round Bolt			15
			56

Rec'd Payment Seam'n Lowerre
R A Knees

Mr Dusenbury

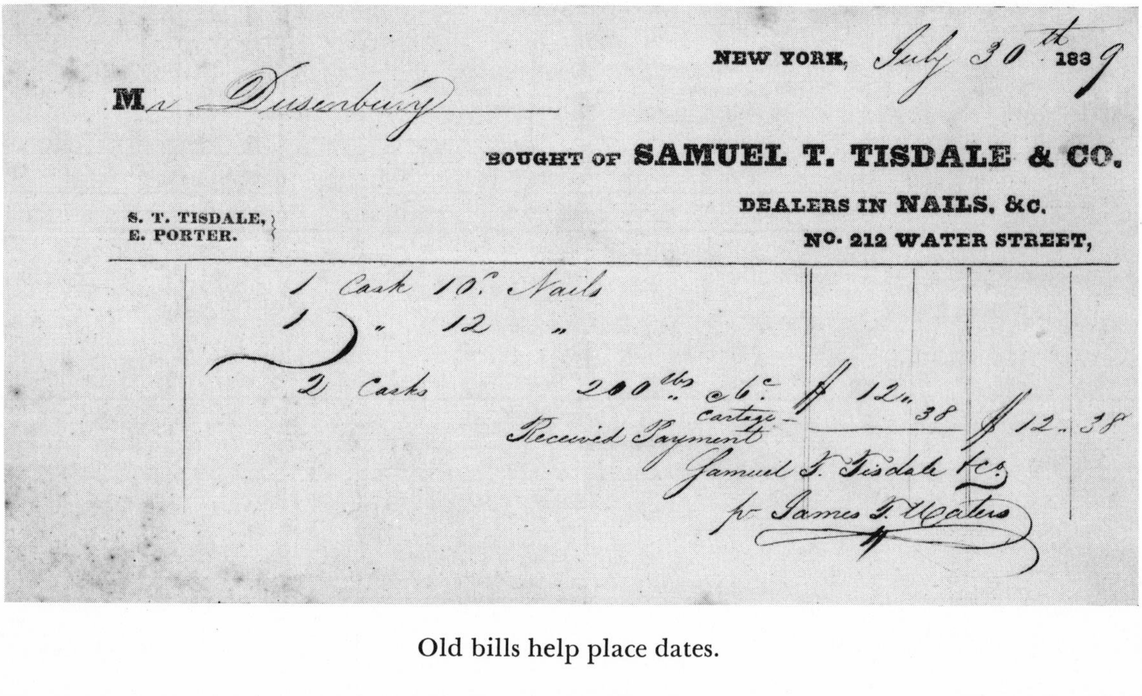

NEW YORK, *July 30th* 183*9*

BOUGHT OF SAMUEL T. TISDALE & CO.

DEALERS IN NAILS, &c.

S. T. TISDALE,
E. PORTER.

NO. 212 WATER STREET,

1 Cask 10d. Nails			
1 " 12 "			
2 Casks 200 lbs 6¢	$12 38	$12 38
cartage		

Received Payment
Samuel T. Tisdale &c.
pr James T. Waters

Old bills help place dates.

ence to the house, while helpful, can never be decisive. So many houses burned down or were blown away and new ones erected on their foundations, and too often public records are non-existent. Quite often a house was built after its ell—and the house dated for its older part. Later houses may sometimes be identified through town records.

Dates affixed to houses may be a guide but they are not always accurate, especially if they have been applied in recent years. Owners are often inclined to be optimistic about the antiquity of their dream house and indulge in a little harmless snobbery. On the other hand, there are a number of well-known cases of houses labelled as being fifty or seventy-five year *younger* than they actually were! This happened in the old days when some new owner acquired the place and made it over. The only important date to him was the year it had become his home, and he set the figures in a plaster panel on the masonry gable or on the chimney, or used iron numerals, or cut them into the fireplace lintel or even inscribed them over the door.

One of the most interesting features of the Pennsylvania stone farmhouses are date panels. These are found in a variety of locations and in a variety of materials and design. Sometimes only a date was used; sometimes a date and initials; more rarely, a date and name, or names of the husband and wife who built the house. The date panel might even be embellished with the symbolic star, tulip or heart, painted or carved. Their location might be high up on the gable wall, between windows on a front wall, or door lintels, or occupying the center of a pedimented gable over the front door. These decorations were sometimes painted on plaster or wood, molded in cast iron, or carved or painted on door lintels of wood or stone. Occasionally they are featured on an exterior wall of stone by being placed in a recessed panel, or formed of burned brick.

In one house we helped date, the figures 1716 were carved in a beam set in the chimney base. The beam turned out to have been salvaged from a house wrecked in a storm several years before the house was built and since stored in a barn. We had to wade through a hide trunk full of old letters and bills to find that out.

Even an old map that shows a house where yours now stands cannot be accepted as conclusive evidence that this was the same house. As a matter of fact, apart from documents, no one thing can be relied upon in dating most houses. The evidence needs to be built up from a number of minor indications, such as the kind of nails used, the hardware patterns, the window glass and the sash, the fireplaces, chimney and bake oven location—in fact everythng from the composition of the walls and the plaster to the architectural details such as panel moldings. Even then it is necessary to take into account the location of the house. The farther east and the nearer the originally populated areas, the earlier new materials and innovations would have been adopted. In backwoods sections, old methods and old materials would naturally be used long after they had been abandoned in more settled communities. For instance, the adventurous pioneers who journeyed to the Western Reserve naturally built the type of home with which they were most familiar in New England. That is why we find so many "Connecticut farmhouses" in Ohio, built many years after their prototypes in the East.

Telltale features of old windows—wavy glass, small panes.

When you get to know old houses you can size them up pretty quickly. Looking at the house first from the outside, you observe the general type, its proportions and construction. In the case of a leanto house, for example, you would see whether the chimney was square or oblong, whether or not it was located behind the ridge, whether it appeared to be original and of what it was built. If it was of stone, oblong, and behind the ridge you would conclude that the place was very old indeed. Then you would probably look behind the chimney to see if another flue had been added there, evidence of a later addition of a kitchen in the leanto.

Next you might observe the windows which can tell quite a lot. The older the house, the smaller the panes will be (providing they are the originals); the glass will look very old and have an opalescent tinge, and its surface will be quite wavy. The sash may be of the guillotine type (vertical sliding, but without counterweights) as introduced in the East, in 1715. This sash will have a very light frame with comparatively heavy muntins (the bars that separate the sheets of glass) with the glass set flush, making the tiny panes seem even smaller. These broad muntins (one and one-quarter inches to one and one-half inches) were common around 1780, by which time many of the old "twelve over eights" and "nine over six" sashes had been replaced

88

by larger-paned windows. Normally, the earlier the house, the smaller the windows, depending somewhat, of course, on the social status of the owner.

In these early houses with their odd-sized sash, the upper sash either did not open at all, or could be dropped only a few inches. The lower sash, on the contrary, could be raised to fully open position. Making this lower sash smaller, therefore, rendered it easier to lift in a day when such windows did not have any counterbalancing weights.

"Keeping up with the Joneses" seems to have been a matter of concern to home owners even in those early days. At least, very many of the old houses had their original windows replaced with ones having larger lights. This was especially true after 1770, when panes as large as 8 x 10 inches were becoming generally available, though not manufactured in this country till 1792 and therefore quite expensive.

An interesting sidelight is thrown on the trend toward larger window panes by the practice of painting the putty dark—an idea that was introduced just before the Revolution. This made the muntins seem more slender and the panes larger. The colors used were first, red, made from red lead; then indigo, a mixture of blue, white, and black.

In many houses built in the late 17th or early 18th Centuries the original windows were all either of the fixed or casement type, having tiny panes set in lead. The windows that these houses have today, therefore, are substitutions, some of them converted in 1775 or later. Students of history will recall that many of the early leaded windows were sacrificed to make bullets during the Revolutionary war—an indica-

On old Pennsylvania stone houses, solid-panelled shutters are a standard feature.

tion that considerable numbers of them had survived to that late date. In this same period, many houses that originally had only one window each side of the front door got more light and air in by adding another one. After about 1792, the fashion was to have twelve-light windows—six to each sash. Luckily, many owners could not afford such an unappealing extravagance.

One of the most striking features of stone house interiors is the practice of installing drawers in window bottoms. Many of the early window openings were made quite tall. The window frame then had a deep—perhaps six to eight inches—bottom rail.

With the window bottom extending below the chair rail, the rail molding was carried down with it across the window. A drawer was located in this recessed space by setting a board in the stone window bottom, and another one above it at chair rail height. These were spaced apart by a narrow board set on edge at each side, completing the boxlike opening. Into this opening a drawer was fitted. (Fig. 89.) This practice was apparently common as far back as the early 1700s.

In rooms where there is no chair rail, the windows still may have a drawer, and sometimes the drawer will be several inches narrower than the window opening, for some obscure reason. In either case, the inside edges of the window may be set off with a wooden trim—a 1 x 4-inch board molded on both edges, that runs up both sides and across the top—inside the reveal.

These window openings are almost always topped by a two-inch oak plank, though a flat stone is sometimes used in the very early houses. This board soffit will probably be painted over or covered thickly with layers of whitewash. The outside edge of the opening will most likely be supported by heavy oak timbers (about 3 x 4 inches) forming the window frame, either flush with the front wall or set in an inch or so.

The Palladian windows, as used on Georgian style houses, were introduced about 1749, and will be found on houses built as late as 1790. By that time it had become the fashion to use a triple window without the taller arched central head that identified Palladio's brain-child. Dormer windows also throw some light on age. The earliest are those of the shed variety found on gambrel roofs before 1700. Toward the middle of the 18th Century, the simple peak-roofed (dog-house) dormer was introduced, having a rectangular window with a gable above it. With the classic influence beginning to assert it-

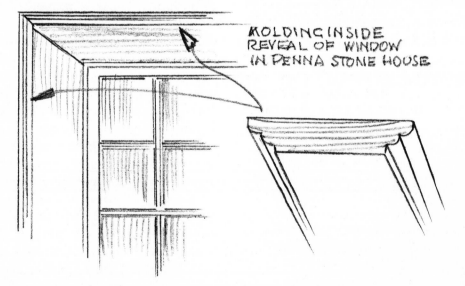

MOLDING INSIDE REVEAL OF WINDOW IN PENNA STONE HOUSE

(a) Pennsylvania stone house.

These three drawings show typical early window-molding.

90

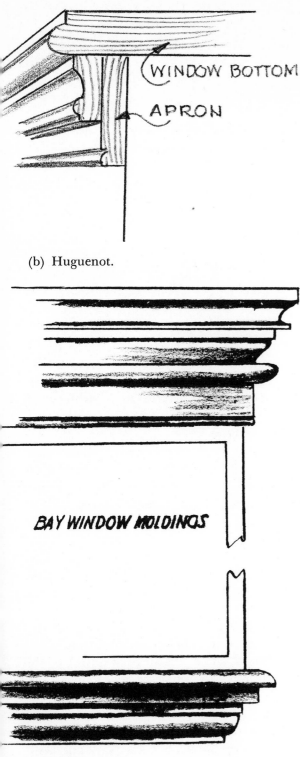

(b) Huguenot.

BAY WINDOW MOLDINGS

(c) Williamsburg.

self in even the smaller houses (1740 or so) these gables became full-fledged triangular pediments. By 1745, the arched-roof dormer had also appeared, and both types were often used together on the larger houses.

Returning to the subject of standard sash windows, not until the late 19th Century were both sashes made fully openable. That meant that each had to be fitted with some device to keep them open at varying heights. The earliest of such devices applied to any kind of window was a peg stuck through a hole in the inside edge of the sash into a corresponding hole in the frame. The peg was usually kept handy by being hung on a thong or string from the frame. Later on, a spring-operated peg was used and continued to be popular well into the 19th Century. This was operated by pulling its metal plunger outward. Another early type of stop consisted of a flat, stepped plunger with a shoulder that fitted into notches cut into the edge of the sash. A third early type has a little curved lever that is pushed up to release the sash. In all cases, these fittings were first applied to one side of the sash only. In the later 19th Century it became common practice to use these fittings in pairs, unless the windows were counterbalanced and fitted with sash locks. Counterbalancing the sash with weights was first suggested in the middle of the 18th Century, but since it involved constructing a box frame around the sashes it did not gain much favor till the 19th Century—at least on the smaller houses. In Victorian times, many an old house was modernized by replacing the old windows with these weighted sashes and frames, a change that may be revealed by examining the adjacent studs.

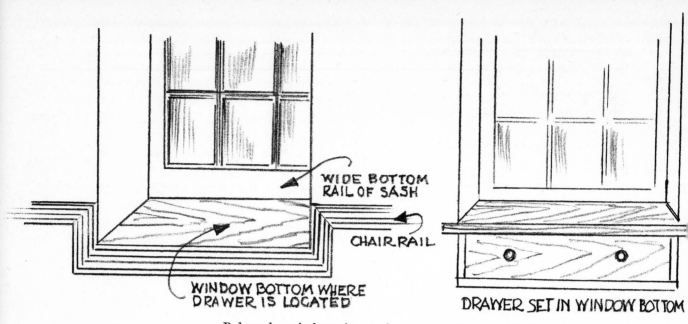

WIDE BOTTOM RAIL OF SASH

CHAIR RAIL

WINDOW BOTTOM WHERE DRAWER IS LOCATED

DRAWER SET IN WINDOW BOTTOM

Below the windows in southern stone houses may be found built-in drawers or lined recesses. (Figs. 88 & 89).

Shutters and Blinds

Solid shutters and louvered blinds on old houses are no particular guide to age, though there are some important exceptions. Practically all houses that had large, fixed windows or the later guillotine windows were originally equipped with solid shutters, both to protect the glass and to discourage potential intruders. These shutters were mostly of batten construction on the smaller houses, but by 1720 the Dutch had already begun to use panelled shutters. Similar shutters, some of rather elaborate construction, were also used by the Huguenots in the Hudson Valley and farther south, by the Germans in Pennsylvania.

As the classical influence began to be felt, panelled shutters on the larger houses were given fancy moldings. At this time louvered blinds began to take the place of shutters, though some householders apparently were content simply to do away with shutters. These blinds had fixed louvers, and the later type with adjustable louvers did not come into general use before 1800 or thereabouts. Even then, solid shutters were retained on the majority of masonry houses. Blinds were also used on the front doors of houses after 1800, and these were of the fixed-slat type.

In quite a few of the houses where extra windows were added, blinds could not be used between pairs of windows without overlapping. This led to many of the blinds being left off, and they should not be reinstalled in restorations. In cases where houses do not have blinds or shutters at the present time, these should not be added until thorough investigation shows that they were once fitted. The only excuse for a great many of them is that they improve the appearance of the house architecturally; they do not add to the air of antiquity or its authenticity. In replacing any shutters or blinds, care must be taken to see that they are the exact size and are hung so that they could be used if necessary. Unless they are actually functional they are fakes and will look it!

SHUTTER CONSTRUCTION
(inside)

How a Huguenot window shutter was put together.

Exterior Doors

Exterior doors and doorways also show a progressive trend that may indicate approximate dates. Dutch doors have been used since the early 17th Century. The earliest were made of a pair of wide planks, sometimes held together with battens, but more often with vertical pieces between the battens to form a frame. This produced a panel effect on the inside, and the upper half of the door might have a bull's-eye glass let into the center of this square. Many of these doors had wooden hinges.

The early 18th Century Dutch doors often had raised panels, and were lined with horizontal boards. Sometimes a pair of bull's-eye lights appeared in the uppermost panels. Later, in 1730, or so, when it became the fashion to install transom lights over the door, the panes in the door itself

Five designs of shutter catches from the Hudson River Valley.

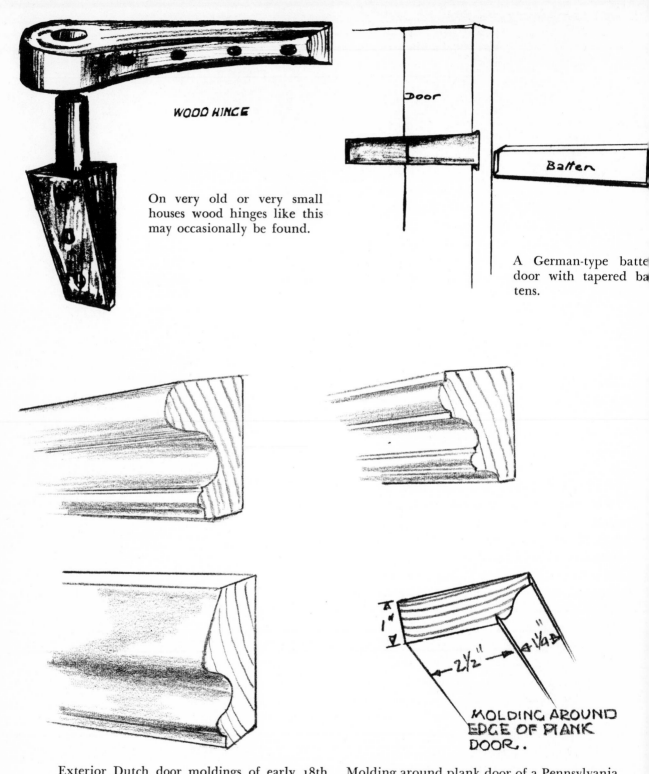

WOOD HINGE

On very old or very small houses wood hinges like this may occasionally be found.

Door

Batten

A German-type batter door with tapered battens.

Exterior Dutch door moldings of early 18th Century.

MOLDING AROUND EDGE OF PLANK DOOR.

Molding around plank door of a Pennsylvania farmhouse.

were eliminated. These raised panels would be set in thick stiles and rails, perhaps with a thin bead to outline the sunken backs of the panels.

At about the time of the Revolution, these doors were made with sunken panels but still retained the bead molded on the rails and stiles. The separate molding to hold the panel in was introduced shortly thereafter. These doors, also, were lined with horizontal sheathing boards. In both northern and southern colonies, the earliest single doors were made of pairs of vertical planks lined with horizontal boards held by a couple of hundred hand-forged nails clinched into the back. (On one door we counted two hundred and twenty-four such nails!) In Pennsylvania, some of these exterior doors were three boards thick so that the inside planks ran in the same direction as the outside ones—vertically! On the more important houses, these plank doors sometimes have a molding around the outside edge which gives them quite a distinguished air. A typical molding is shown.

The door frames, in most areas, at first consisted of plain stiles and top rail. By 1700, lights in the top of the door were common, as were raised panels. During the first quarter of the 18th Century, the door surrounds began to take on added dignity. On the wooden house, a simple shelf or drip board became a cornice, then gradually developed into a complete pediment, with the door stiles becoming pilasters to support it.

In the masonry houses, the opening in the wall was often enlarged upward to accommodate either a single or double row of lights. The door frames, together with the lights would, as a rule, be flush with the front of the wall, with the door itself

An attractive front door hood on a Pennsylvania stone house.

recessed six inches or so, depending on the thickness of the masonry.

By the middle of the 18th Century, in both wooden and masonry houses, the door surround was generally more classical in design, with broken pediments in high favor. In the masonry houses these door surrounds sometimes spread themselves over the outside of the walls so that the entrance acquired a far greater importance than formerly. Doors in general were larger, and in the case of wooden center-chimney houses they often had of necessity to be made double. The wider single door would

95

not swing fully open in the shallow space between the front wall and the staircase. In recent times we have come across two instances of a wide single door being substituted for the old double door, with unfortunate results. In such a case the door stiles should be examined for evidences of hinges on both sides.

Interior Doors

Dating a house by means of its interior doors is no easy task. So many things have to be taken into consideration—the kind of wood and the way it is worked, the size of the pieces, and how they are put together. Normally we think of the batten door as being the earliest type, but panelled doors go back to 1700 on the better-class house and batten doors were used in the 20th Century.

The earliest example of a panelled door for a small house that we know of goes back to 1687 or earlier—it is believed. This was a two-panelled door. The top panel was made of two boards and the lower one of three, and none of them was square (Fig. 95.) Most of the very early panelled doors have raised panels that project beyond the

(very early panelled door)
(1687)

A two-panel door of 1687. Fig. 95.

were chamfered on the front face so that when they were inserted in the grooves in the frame they projected a quarter of an inch beyond the face of the frame at the front and were recessed a quarter of an inch at the back.

In later panelled doors, say from the last quarter of the 18th Century, the panels

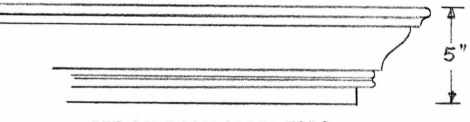

INTERIOR ROOM DOORHEADS

Huguenot interior room doorheads.

level of the stiles and rails. Both frame and panels would be made of wood seven-eighths of an inch to one-inch thick. The panels

would be made of wood a quarter of an inch thinner than the frames. This meant that the panels were flush with the frames

96

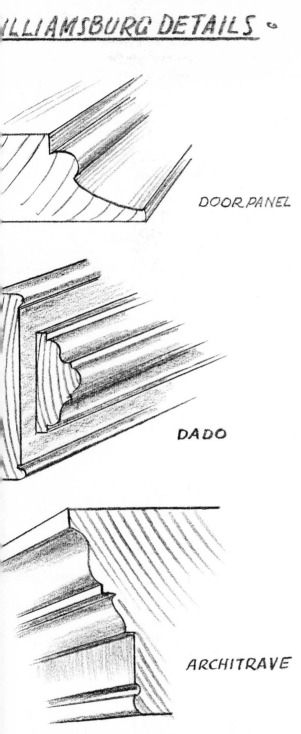

DOOR PANEL

DADO

ARCHITRAVE

Williamsburg interior trim details.

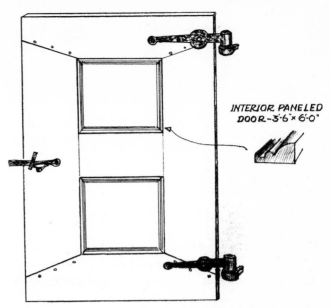

INTERIOR PANELED
DOOR - 3'-6" × 6'-0"

Panelled interior door of early 18th-Century Huguenot house.

at the front. Still later, probably after the Revolution, flush-panel doors, with panels that were beaded but not chamfered, came into general use. These, too, were sunk slightly at the back. The big difference between the early raised-panel doors and the later ones was the fact that the panel bead was at first a part of the frame. Later, these beads were applied after the panel was inserted—strips of quarter-round or ovolo molding. In a great many houses panelled doors are used for the better rooms, and batten doors for kitchen, cellar, and attic.

Interior Panelling

Panelling is very often a guide because that too was a victim of fashion. First the completely panelled rooms of the 17th and early 18th Centuries. Then the general shrinkage of interior woodwork—first to the fireplace wall, then to a mere wainscot, chair-rail high, as plastered walls became popular. There seems to be no distinction

97

as to date between sunk and raised panels. In the 17th Century the sunk panel was in vogue and probably much cheaper than the raised type. Then there are two types of raised panel, one of which is earlier than the other—and these are much easier to

Fireplace wall and door panelling of a 1720 New England "saltbox." Figs. 99 and 100. (*Courtesy Miss Janie Pierce*)

Stair panelling and rail from a 1720 "saltbox. (*Courtesy Miss Janie Pierce*)

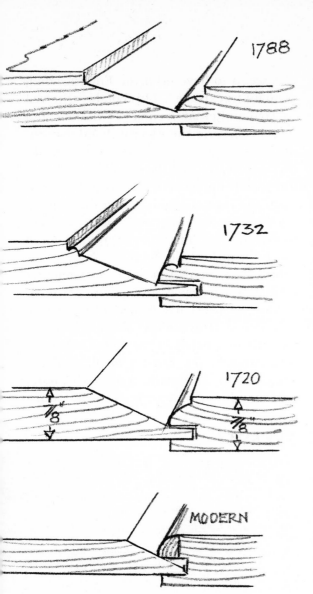

1788

1732

1720

MODERN

Varieties of early panelling.

picture than to describe! (Figs. 100 and 102.) There were also interesting variations in the frame molding on stiles or rails, but these may be due to individual taste more than period. Usually the plainer the panel, the earlier it is.

Clapboarding

Another external feature that throws some light on the age of a wooden house is the siding. As we mentioned earlier, very early clapboards were short (four to six feet), thick, and carefully jointed by bevelling the ends. This practice was continued until about 1800 on the better constructed houses. The graduation of the clapboards by increasing the exposure seems to have been a fad that lasted probably from 1740 to 1750 or a little later. After 1750 it became common practice to install sheathing under the clapboards, but there are many exceptions. At about this same time, the vogue for the hewn overhang seems to have died out.

The Universal Brick

In New Amsterdam, the Albany area, New England and Virginia bricks were made in the early 17th Century, and the size of the bricks and the manner in which they were laid are a guide to their origin and period. The early sun-dried bricks were used only for wall nogging and were usually very light in color, the tint depending on the original clay. For the most part they were also somewhat larger than the later kiln-dried brick.

The early "English" brick averaged about 8½x4x2⅝, though in Virginia those of 9x3⅜x2⅜ were more common. The early Dutch brick were mostly 8x4x2½, but as time went on the bricks were made somewhat smaller. The names "English" and "Dutch" as used here refer to the standard brick sizes, not the country of their origin. Few, if any, bricks were ever imported.

In many areas the brick sizes were decided upon by the individual brick makers. In the Delaware Valley, for instance, bricks as large as 9½x4½x2¾ are sometimes encountered, but elsewhere in the Middle Colonies they range from 6½x2⅞x1⅝ to

$8\frac{3}{8} \times 4\frac{1}{4} \times 2\frac{3}{8}$. The color of the bricks was of course much more constant. In the Albany area, the Dutch made a brick of a distinct yellow color in the late 17th and early 18th Centuries, and some of these were shipped to Delaware. In Maryland and Virginia, the bricks were of a deep red, while Connecticut Valley clay produced brick of a delightful pink. Much, of course, depended upon the degree of burning. Brick burned at too high a temperature—those exposed to the actual flames—often became partly glazed a deep blue-black. These burned bricks were commonly used as a decorative feature in brick walls. The Dutch actually invented a brick bond to take advantage of this, called the Dutch cross bond.

The earliest brick bonding in the colonies seems to have been the English bond, as might be expected. This bond is achieved by laying alternate courses of headers and stretchers. Later the Flemish bond, consisting of alternate headers and stretchers in each course, became the more popular. Unfortunately not much reliance can be placed upon the type of bond as a means of judging dates, even at that early day. One very well-known 16th-Century Virginia house was built in Flemish bond.

Still later, an American or Common bond was developed, using one course of headers for every five courses of stretchers. The famed Dutch Cross bond, which apparently originated in the 16th Century, is a variation of the English bond, with the stretchers in alternate courses breaking joints with one another (i.e. the joints

ENGLISH

FLEMISH

COMMON

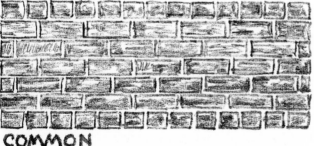

DUTCH

Brick bonding used in old American houses.

were not in line). The result is that the bricks seem to form a series of steps, half a header wide, in both directions down the wall. The effect is that of a diamond or diaper pattern which can be strengthened by picking out the mortar joints or using glazed headers.

This form of decoration was fully developed in Maryland, where an all-header bond was also developed, and is quite common in lower New Jersey. The practice may have originated in Holland or England (where it is called black diapering), or both, but we know of no instance where it was used after 1740.

Nails and Hardware

One of the clues to house dates that fashion is not likely to have changed lies in the kind of nails used to hold the place together. The oldest nails are the hand-forged ones, square, long, and sharply pointed, with a roughly flattened head. In the 17th Century they were imported, but in the early 1700s most people made their own from nail rods—long strips of soft iron.

These nails were in use throughout the 18th Century, and in some areas as long as 1840. Usually, however, you can count on a house in which such nails are used throughout—or at least in the floors and siding—as being built before 1800. The reason for continuing the use of hand-forged nails after the machine cut or "cold" nails were available was that the pure, soft iron withstood clinching. Such nails could also be driven through oak floors and into oak timbers without corroding away in a few years. The harder cut nails could not be bent without cracking and they could not withstand the acids in oak. Even today you will often find that old, hand-made nails

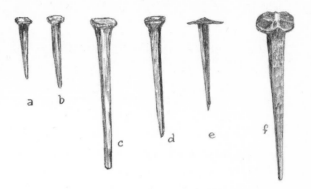

Old nails are a guide to dating—shown left to right are, (a) machine-made brad, (b) hand-made brad, (c) machine-headed square nail, (d) hand-headed slit nail, (e) handmade small nail, (f) handmade from nailrods.

An early nail-cutting machine. (*Photo by Essex Institute*)

cannot be pulled out of oak floor joists without breaking.

These are the reasons hand-forged nails are often found clinched in batten doors and used in floors long after they were supposed to have been superseded. Another reason is that such nails were treasured and often handed down from one generation to another. And many a lot of old house timbers has been burned just to salvage the nails. A nail-cutting machine was invented during the last quarter of the 18th Century, but cut nails did not become common in many areas till around the turn of the century. This machine slit the nails out of flat strips of iron, and the strip had to be turned over to finish the cuts. As a consequence, these nails show one rounded edge and one burred edge on each side. Ten years or so later, a newer machine did the job in one stroke, so that the nails had two round and two burred edges adjacent. Another difference was that the head had to be formed by hand on the earlier nails; it was done by the machine on the later ones. The various types are illustrated and dated.

The earlier types of hardware likewise are a good guide to age. The really old houses always had primitive door handles and hinges when they were built. But they may not have them today, either because the owner wanted to keep his house up-to-date or some "junk-snupper" talked him into selling or exchanging them for more modern ones. This often happened in the past sixty years or so, and doubtless before. Nevertheless, it usually pays to examine the hardware in the less accessible places such as the cellars and attics, closets, or even outhouses.

The earliest hinges, apart from the wooden or leather ones, were the iron straps, some of which are delightful in design and proportion. Almost every area has its characteristic designs forged by the local blacksmith—and occasionally found elsewhere, to the confusion of the expert.

These strap hinges were used on both interior and exterior doors in the 17th

A strap hinge of early design from Connecticut. Note eye is not welded. Fig. 106.

Century. On the interior doors they gave way largely to other types in the early 1800s. Although most strap hinges look pretty much alike to the casual observer, there are important differences that tell a story apart from regional variations in design. The early hinges were made both by blacksmiths, and by farmers and others where there were no blacksmiths available. Some of the hinges seem to have been made from old wagon tires, others from flat rolled iron. Some were worked cold, some were hot-forged. Because of these variations, dating is generally difficult.

The crudest type of strap hinge is that made with the "eye" merely wrapped around the pintle, and not welded; considerably better is the welded eye in which the strap material forms a solid ring. In quite late hinges this type might be made by forging a solid, rounded end and drilling the eye through it. A much simpler method was to fold over the end of the strap in a loop, and weld the end to the back, or, less frequently, the front of the strap. (See Fig. 106.) This seems to have been quite an early method, with all the nail holes punched instead of drilled. It is quite easy to tell whether the nail holes have been punched or drilled. If they are drilled, they will be all of the same size, perfectly round, and probably well in line. There will also be signs of a burr on the under-

The cross-garnet or T-hinge popular in Connecticut. Fig. 106a.

side of each hole. With the punch, the underside of the hole will have a flattened area around it.

The earliest strap hinges were hung on a round pin, or pintle, formed with a spike at right angles to it. The spike was intended to be driven into either a masonry joint or a wooden door post. For interior doors, or other positions where a spike was likely to split the wood, the pintle would be formed with a plate for nailing. Such a hinge is likely to be later than the plain pintle-strap, but earlier than the cross-garnet or T-hinge. The latter is somewhat like a strap but is held by a plate having two eyes and a pin. (Fig. 106a.) Another quite early strap hinge is the wrap-around type. In this the attaching plate is slotted and the metal out of the slot bent around to form a spindle. Around this the eye of the strap is forged.

All of these hinges may vary in the design of their finials as well as their general shape. However, apart from the beautiful cock's head hinge from England, the only distinctive ones seem to be those of German (Moravian) and Dutch, and French designs.

An almost universal characteristic of the Dutch types is the large, circular swelling near the eye end. This usually is pierced for four nails, providing extra firm attachment where it is needed most. Some German hinges are long and narrow, with little ears squashed out every few inches along the sides. Some have larger ears, or rounded sections, near the center, with nail holes. The hinges taper from both ends toward this circular part. The German designers

A cock's head hinge from England (a)

also were fond of the fleur-de-lys and pierced finial. The French likewise, and with more reason, used the fleur-de-lys in a variety of treatments.

Another 17th Century hinge that grew exceedingly popular towards 1700 was the dove-tail or "butterfly" hinge, as it came to

and a Dutch version (b).

103

A typical feature of Dutch strap hinges is the circular nailing pad.

be called. This was a pin-type hinge with both halves of a somewhat triangular shape. It was not suitable for heavy doors, and in time its use became confined to cupboards and furniture. Because of its attractive shape, the butterfly hinge is still popular in restoration and reproduction where the original type is not known. The door butterflies were of thick iron, bevelled at the edges, and often decorated with notches. The more fancy ones seem to have been imported from England, and in use they were made even more decorative by the use of red-leather washers under the nail heads. This practice was continued in many areas with the H and HL hinges that were introduced in the early 1700s, and maintained their popularity well into the 19th Century. These, too, especially the decorated ones, were imported in large quantities.

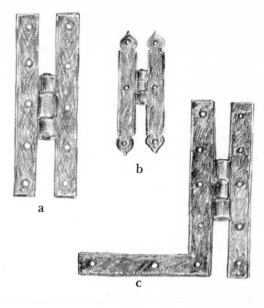

H hinges from (a) Connecticut, (b) Holland, (c) A New England H-L hinge.

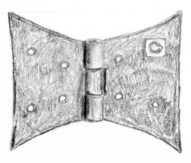

A butterfly hinge.

After about 1770 butt hinges began to be used on doors that were thick enough to take them. The first ones were made of sheet iron, bent double, into two thicknesses, to form the pin loops. Fifteen years later, the uninteresting cast-iron butts were

being made. In country districts, and in houses with batten doors, the H-type hinge retained its popularity. The butt was useless on doors one inch thick or less, and in any case was more difficult to install than the surface hinges. The L of the HL type was especially useful on panelled doors to help keep the corner-joints square. The H, located halfway up the door, held it from warping, whether panelled or battened.

The subject of hinges cannot be left without a note on finish. In the old days, if the hinges were used on unpainted doors, they were left in their natural state. If they were used on painted doors, they were painted the same color as the door. They should be accorded the same treatment today. The rage for painting these hinges black under all circumstances is justified neither by ancient custom nor good taste.

Door Latches

Undoubtedly the most interesting of all house hardware are the door latches. They are, unfortunately, questionable guides to the antiquity of the house, being far too easily added or removed. Nevertheless, their design is usually identifiable and datable, and the various types easily distinguishable.

The earliest door latches were undoubtedly wooden ones, both on interior and exterior doors. But soon the knocker latches came along, first in Virginia, then in New Amsterdam and the Hudson Valley. In both the English and the Dutch styles, the knocker consisted of a loop handle hinged

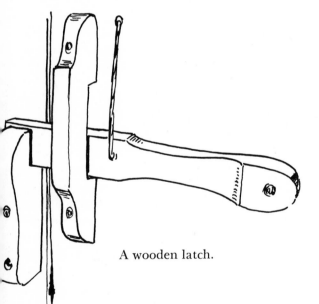

A wooden latch.

to the eye of a heavy split pin passing through the door. Lifting the handle and turning it raised the latch. On the inside of the door the pin moved the latch in one of two ways. In the English type latch, the

split pin extended through a rectangular hole in the end of the latch bar. Turning the handle raised the other end of the bar from behind the catch. In the Dutch-style knocker latch, the pin turned a cam that lifted the bar, this time with a great deal less effort. (Fig. 112.)

Before 1700, however, another type of latch, called the Suffolk latch, was being imported, and local blacksmiths were soon copying them. These are the simple but highly decorative latches that are standard

Lift and catch of early latch.

Dutch knocker-latch. Fig. 112.

equipment on most old houses built before 1785—and on many built after that date. By that time the early pattern Suffolk latch had undergone a change and that is somewhat of a guide to dating.

The original Suffolk latches were all of soft iron, consisting of a loop handle termi-

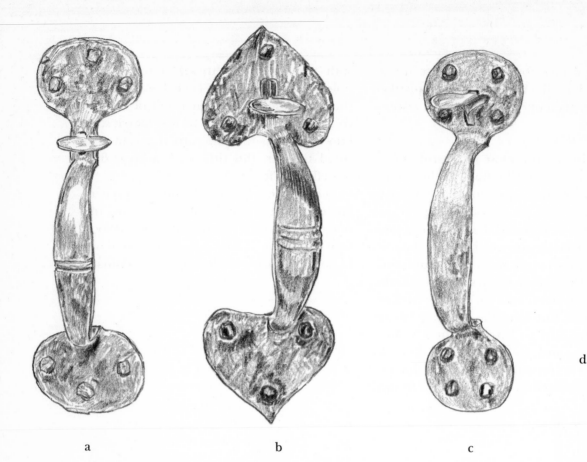

a   b   c

nating top and bottom in separate flat leaves called cusps. Nail holes through these cusps enabled the handle to be fastened to the door. The latch was raised by a "lift"—a straight or curved, flat piece of iron with a flat, circular piece on the outer end called a thumb-press. This lift passed through a hole in the upper cusp, and usually was held from slipping out by a tongue, or a notch, formed in its underside. The bar was held to the back of the door by a nail through one end and a staple at the other end. It dropped into a catch whose spiked end was driven into the door post.

The most interesting feature of these latches is the design of the cusps. In the 18th Century, the commonest designs were the bean, the arrow, heart, ball-and-spear,

d

Popular designs of Suffolk latches. (a) bean swivel, (b) heart cusp, (c) bean cusp, (d) bean swivel, (e) single cusp.

e

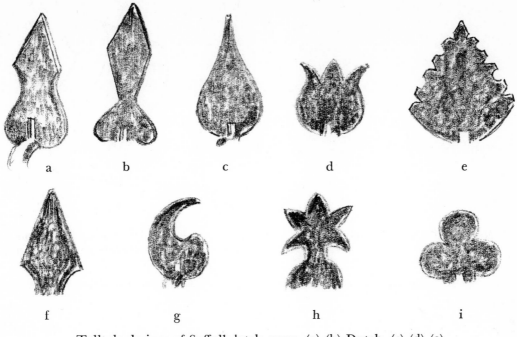

a   b   c   d   e

f   g   h   i

Telltale designs of Suffolk latch cusps. (a) (b) Dutch, (c) (d) (e)
Pennsylvania, (f) New York, (g) (h) Connecticut, (i) New Jersey.

swordfish, and tulip patterns. But there were many others. Common to all the colonies in the early days was the arrow pattern, and the bean design was imported in large quantities. Many of the earlier latches were apparently home-made, with simple oval or leaf-shaped cusps, made in one piece from a round bar. The nail holes were crudely punched. From then on each region developed its favorite patterns.

For the most part, the Pennsylvania latches were made with a round handle, or grasp, in contrast to the flattened or half-round type favored elsewhere. Another Pennsylvania specialty was the handle with a cusp at the top and a spike at the bottom. The spike pierced the door and was clinched over on the inside. Easily spotted are the Moravian (German) designs, mostly angular and prim, on the order of stylized tulip and leaf. Other Pennsylvania areas boasted the teardrop, pear, and pine tree (serrated) pat-terns. An early feature of exterior doors on Pennsylvania farm houses, dating perhaps from the 17th Century, is the scroll-type wooden handle. (Fig. 116.) This is often made of oak and held by two, clinched nails to the lined door. The most lavishly beauti-ful seem to come from New England, in-cluding the swordfish design from the sea coast, a stylized tulip from the Housatonic Valley, and the tobacco leaf. The Dutch in New York had two designs of their own, like spearheads with heart-shaped bases. Smaller patterns were simple—usually oval cusps; the trefoil was indigenous to New Jersey.

The handle designs however are so nu-merous and so varied—and so well-travelled —that it is impossible to be really specific. In checking the original locality of any special piece, therefore, it is best to refer to a standard work on the subject such as Sonn's *Early American Wrought Iron.*

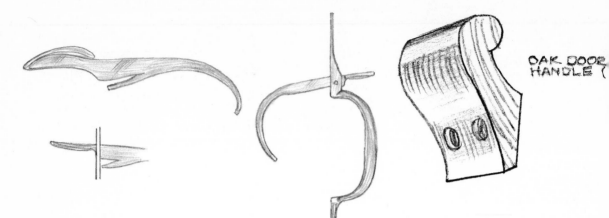

Lifts for Norfolk and Suffolk latches.

Door-pull of wood on a Pennsylvania farmhouse. Fig. 116.

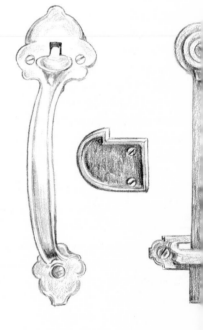

A Norfolk latch created by a blacksmith-artist.

A typical New England **Norfolk** latch.

Blake's Patent Cast-ir Latch of 1840 and on.

There is, however, one definite indication of period in the style of the Suffolk latch. In the early type, current to about 1770, the lift passed through the upper cusp. In the later type, the handle is thickened and slotted just below the upper cusp. The lift passes through this and is held in position by a hinge that passes through it. This type of Suffolk latch continued in use almost halfway through the 19th Century in spite of competition from two other styles—the Norfolk latch and, later, Blake's Patent Cast-Iron Latch.

Some indication of the relative ages of the swivel-lift patterns of Suffolk latches is afforded by the shapes of the thumb presses. The very early latches (1790 +) usually had very thin and flat presses; after 1800 many of the presses were slightly hollowed, and still later ones were both hollowed and curved like a leaf.

The Norfolk latch is distinguished by the fact that the handle is mounted on a back plate. While some quite ornate styles of Norfolk latches were available before 1750, they did not become popular until the later ones did. As a rule, the later the latch the plainer the back plate. In the early 1800s, the back plates were made somewhat thicker, and were drilled with countersunk holes for screws instead of punched holes for nails. As in the case of the Suffolk latches, the later catches, staples, and bars were mounted on back plates. Still later—about 1830—buttons were added to the bars to help lift them from the inside, since the lifts themselves were made very short. And so the Norfolk latch grew in popularity till about 1840 when the industrial age began to make itself felt in the mass-produced cast-iron latch that immortalized the name of Blake.

Keeping Out Intruders

Throughout the 18th Century the householder's favorite method of securing the outside doors against intrusion was with a stout oak bar dropped into iron hooks and staples. A lot of these have survived to this day, but from 1740 on, the iron bolt began to grow in favor. In the case of small bolts, the earlier ones were held with staples, later ones were mounted on back plates. The larger bolts, used at the tops and bottoms of doors, had to be mounted on plates so that the widely spaced staples would remain in line, and sufficient friction be maintained to hold them either in or out. These are found on houses dating as far back as 1700, but they were far from common then. Sketches show the commoner types you are likely to encounter.

Chapter VI

Restoration Procedures

IN PLANNING the restoration of an old house, it is both interesting and useful to know what style of house it originally was. The fact that it looks like a Greek Revival today may mean little or nothing. It may have been a center-chimney Early American brought up to date in the early 1900s with a new door and porch; with two-story pilasters applied over the old corner boards; with the gables extended into a fancy overhang; and triangular, diamond, square, or oval windows let into the gables, or pediments mounted over the windows. Or, it may have been a two-story Early American transformed into a stately Southern Georgian by adding a portico to the front, with two-story pillars supporting a flat roof attached to the front of the original eaves. The important thing, therefore, is to examine a house critically—especially if it is one of the later hybrids—separating the old features from the newer and discovering what is basic and what is a later face-lifting development. A study of the characteristic features of each type of house will help here.

The second thing to be decided may be whether or not "it will pay" to restore, or even remodel this particular house. In doing this the proud owner—actual or po-

tential—usually takes into consideration the historical or sentimental value of the place as well as its financial worth. In only one instance have we been called upon to give an adverse opinion in such a case. This involved a large house that had lost much of its roof in a windstorm, and all of the central chimney from the attic floor up. Apart from this, there was extensive rot in the timbers and window frames, and much of the siding was in poor condition. Considerable alterations had been made to the interior, and a small brick chimney built up alongside the original one, passing up through the main floor, close to a fireplace. The main fireplace with its bake oven had collapsed; several ceilings were down; and the floor of the entry was rotted through.

The original house seemed to date from the late 18th Century, and except for the added chimney, had not been modernized. It was quite clear that it would cost more to repair the house than it would be worth in cash after the restoration was finished. However, the owner decided the cost was secondary, and enough of the original house would be left to form the nucleus of what could be an attractive old-time home. And when we thought of instances we had encountered of eighty thousand to one

An antique house delightfully restored.
(*Courtesy Howard C. Sherwood*)

hundred thousand dollars being spent to reproduce with old materials a house not worth more than half that amount in the open market, we were forced to agree.

What this all amounts to, therefore, is that whether a house is worth restoring or not depends on the house and its owner—a matter of personal predilection. For most of us, on the other hand, such a decision must be an economically sound one, so that we can at least expect to salvage most of our investment should the need arise. In this respect the old houses have the advantage over new ones; their value increases with time, providing they are not neglected. It is of course essential in mak-

ing such a decision that the house first be carefully analyzed, and the requirements for putting it approximately in its original condition closely estimated. In doing this, we need to differentiate between the various features that constitute its appeal—those that represent original construction, and therefore have antiquarian value—and those architectural features that give it character and make it more desirable as a home of distinction or merely quiet charm.

In the first of these may be included elements of the basic structure—in wooden houses, the original, or at least very old siding, probably with the hand-made nails; in masonry houses, the original brick or

Goodbye—old house.

stonework; and in both cases, the original frame and roof timbers; the old chimney with its fireplaces and bake oven, if any; the panelling or trim or built-in cupboards; the original plaster or old floor boards, original hardware, the old window sash and glass, and so on. The second group of features would cover a great many period changes such as later additions, leantos, etc.; conversions to a later style such as added pilasters or pillars and formal doors, tall windows, moldings applied to original trim, improvements to fireplaces, added windows, extended eaves, panelled interior doors replacing the older battened type, etc.

As a rule, most people usually desire to retain the old features even though they may be more primitive than they like. On the other hand you may find that someone else has already perpetrated an amateur job of restoration and done more harm than good. For example, there seems to be an almost universal conviction that crudity and antiquity are synonymous. That is the

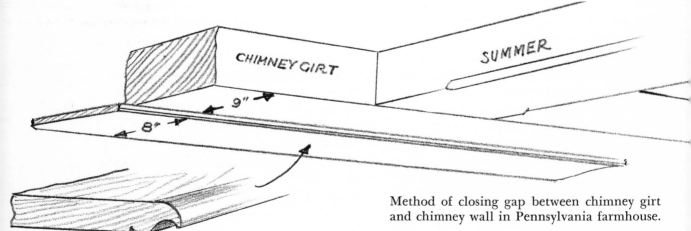

Method of closing gap between chimney girt and chimney wall in Pennsylvania farmhouse.

112

reason we find so many interiors ruined by post and beam casings being removed to expose the ax-marked timbers. No house was ever built that way. The old-time carpenters and joiners went to great pains to finish off all exposed woodwork, and when rough timbers were used in exposed positions — such as corner posts and ceiling beams and joists—these were carefully hidden with smoothly finished boards, nicely beaded or chamfered.

Beam and Post Casings

Here, then, is one common problem—what to do with ax-marked beams robbed of their casings? If the casing boards can be found they should be put back where they belong. But more often than not they have been cut up for shelving, or firewood! The problem then is to find old boards that can be used in their place. Usually these need to be no more than five-eighths or three-quarters of an inch thick. The second problem is to find old nails to put them on with —the search centering on cellar, attic, or even pantry, where such nails may have been used for hanging things. If possible, the boards should be jointed as shown in the sketch.

Removing Old Paint

Another diabolical practice that has to be contended with in restoration is that of stripping down the woodwork regardless of authenticity. This seems to be a universal urge. Time and again we have watched new owners of old houses busily scraping off paint even though the ceilings were half down and the floorboards missing. However, there is some excuse, for nothing looks better than a nice, old pine interior. Unfortunately a lot of this woodwork—especially after 1750 or so—was definitely made to be painted and always has been painted, and something is lost when the paint is removed, even if it is just that little extra tone of formality that paint provides. Taking off the paint actually amounts to remodeling—not restoring. And here we may suggest the modern fad—enthusiastically promoted by lumber dealers who would otherwise have a lot of waste wood on their hands—of using "knotty pine," painted or plain, for walls and trim. Nothing does more to spoil an otherwise authentic interior, for no self-respecting old-time carpenter would use it.

Another reason for "hastening slowly" in removing paint is that it was common practice in the old days to use a variety of woods for trim and panelling that was to be painted. Basswood, butternut, elm and others were mixed with the pine, and many a panel had a knot or two if it was to be painted. Just as the joiners covered ax-marked posts so did they paint over the mixed and poorer-quality woods. Therefore, in restoration it pays to find out, if possible, whether or not the wood was always painted.

Quite often in the case of panelling you can get at the rear of it, particularly in the case of bedroom rear-walls and fireplace walls. Then there are sometimes cupboards or closets that afford a similar opportunity for inspection. In other cases, some of the woodwork can be removed without damage, failing which, we may be reduced to scraping off small patches of paint, in inconspicuous places, to examine the wood underneath. This process at the same time reveals the number of coats of paint applied and their colors, and may suggest that the wood was never bare. If the bottom layer of paint turns out to be a very hard gray or blue-gray, attempts to strip the wood down further should be abandoned. That base coating is certainly very old—and very hard to remove without damaging the surface of the wood.

If the stripping down is done slowly and carefully, preferably with a putty knife that is not sharp enough to take off two coats at once or dig its corner into the wood, you may make some interesting discoveries. One of the colors may be particularly exciting, or a finish may obviously have been secured by using a glaze over a ground color, producing a transparent effect. Another thing to look for is evidence of painted decoration such as stenciling or graining. Such decorating will probably not date earlier than 1775, and most likely will be after 1800. Even so, every effort should be made to preserve it for its antiquarian value.

One thing you have to remember, in stripping down the panels and trim, is that it is often quite impossible to get rid of all traces of paint without removing the surface of the wood. This is especially true of soft pine as well as of open-grain woods such as oak. The surface has a whitish cast due to paint in the pores, and no remover will draw it out. The fibers have to be sanded or scraped off, destroying the wonderful patina that characterizes very old wood and cannot be duplicated except by exposure and rubbing for many a year. The nearest you can come to that patina is a satiny sheen supplied by light waxing, over a thin wash of white shellac. Very little wax with a bees-wax base and lots of elbow grease will give the best results. But the surface must be the same all over—remnants of paint will show up worse than ever!

In cases where it is decided to leave the bare wood, no treatment actually is necessary. In the majority of instances the wood was left in its original raw condition to mellow with age and dust. In parlors and better rooms where a more finished appearance was wanted, the wood might be given a wiping over with raw linseed oil (which must have taken a long time to dry) then lightly waxed. In theory, of course, it would have been better to use the quicker-drying boiled oil. However, unless we insist on being absolutely authentic in our restoration methods, we can get a much more mellow finish quickly by applying a thin coat of white shellac before waxing. Ordinary four-pound or five-pound shellac must have an equal quantity of grain alcohol added to it, so that it will soak into the grain and not stay on the surface.

Sometimes in matching original wood with old but lighter colored boards or panels, we add a little burnt umber to the shellac. Then a light waxing will produce that dull sheen that gives old wood a wonderful mellow gleam in the candlelight. But use a wax with a bees-wax base such as *Butcher's*. Floors treated in this way need to be kept well waxed.

Interior Painting

In the case of painted interior woodwork, any of the existing old colors can of course be used, depending on how far back in the house's history you wish to go. Actually, removing several layers of paint to get down to one particular layer is a tremendous job and rarely worth the effort in dealing with a complete room.

Paint was used for the interiors of small houses late in the first quarter of the 18th Century, and then may have been confined to baseboards and wainscoting. Baseboards, so vulnerable to dirt, often were given a coat of black or dark red paint, the band of color also being applied to the bottoms of the doors. Later, more of the woodwork was painted, including the pegboards that served for so long in lieu of clothes closets. In very early houses this color was most likely to be the dark Venetian red, made from burned yellow ochre which turned red in the process, and skim milk, with a little soot or lampblack added. In England this color was called Indian red because it was imported from the East Indies. The name has nothing to do with American Indians.

Theoretically, if you want to restore old paintwork you should use the old materials. This has been done quite successfully in a number of cases, but a lot of work is involved besides that needed to apply the stuff. The advantage of doing this is that you actually do duplicate the appearance of the old paint, something that cannot be done exactly with modern pigments and vehicles. In many instances the paint was finished with a glaze or semi-transparent coat that allowed enough of the base color to filter through to produce a marvelous effect of depth. One way of duplicating this is to go over the paint with a thin wash coat of varnish to which a small amount of color has been added, but better results will be obtained by using the whites of eggs instead of varnish. For so-called antiquing, the paint surface is given a smear of color in turpentine, then wiped off in the high spots to give a shaded effect. When that is thoroughly dry it can be given a thinned coating of dull varnish and a light waxing.

Just prior to the middle of the 18th Century, colored paints became more generally available. But since they were expensive—the skim milk and strong beer having given way to turpentine and linseed oil—only the better houses received the benefit. That is why the Georgian houses of this period began to exhibit lovelier interiors in blues, greens, yellows, and grays. Contrasting colors were used in the same rooms, particularly in the South where panels were painted a different tone from their stiles and rails.

This set the fashion for painting everything paintable in the farmhouse type of house, still using the old-type paints. The blue-gray that the amateur restorers of today find so persistent was universally admired as a wainscot and door paint. It appears to have been made of white lead (made by immersing sheet lead in chamber lye), lampblack, and Prussian blue. Today, luckily, a great many of the old-time colors are available in modern paints.

Exterior Painting

One of the most interesting of restoration jobs is the restoring of exterior woodwork to its original color. This is one place in which it is worth while to scrape down the paint to the bottom layer, or, in the case of a wooden house, to lift a clapboard to find traces of old paint in the joints.

The earliest exterior color for wood was red, but white soon became fashionable, so much so that those who could not afford an all-white house, painted the front white and left the rest in the cheaper red. Stone and brick houses sometimes were given a white or yellow wash in the early 1700s.

White paint seems to have been used on Pennsylvania houses very early, and white trim with green blinds and shutters was a popular combination in towns as far apart as Boston, Philadelphia, and Annapolis. There were, of course, individualists who painted their exterior woodwork pumpkin yellow, Spanish brown, stone yellow, a gray "freestone" color, or cream. The choice in many areas was wide, but some of the colors were by no means attractive and therefore should not be used today. There is such a thing as being too authentic when there are the changing fashions of two hundred years to choose from! By the end of the 18th Century, white woodwork and green shutters were standard throughout the country.

What to Do With Floors

In most old-time rooms the floors are responsible for much of the antique flavor. Therefore, in restoring them the principal problem is to preserve their character which is compounded of texture and color and subtle variations of surface resulting from long wear and use. As a last resort in trying to get an unmarred and not too deeply worn surface (and sometimes as the first rash step in that direction) the boards are turned over. The results are never exciting. Old floors do need attention when they are badly warped, when they are much worn between the high spots preserved by the nails; when they are gashed with a firewood axe, or the surface chewed up as though horses had been stabled on them. Nevertheless, in restoration the impulse to re-lay the boards should be resisted till all other methods have proved fruitless.

If the boards are of oak, some will probably be damaged, if not broken in the taking up. The nails will be rusted and can neither be removed nor pulled through. With the softer pine, the nail heads need to be clipped off so they can be pulled through when the board is lifted, but the board may still crack or split. All except the very earliest floor boards will have joints that seal the gap between them, unless shrinkage is severe. These joints increase the liability of damage in removing boards unless the proper procedure is followed. The three commonest joints are (a) shiplap, where each board overlaps the next three quarters of an inch or so; (b) a spline or loose-tongue joint in which the boards have grooves in each edge into which a separate strip of wood is fitted, and (c), the tongue-and-groove joint. The shiplap joint as applied to floors appears to be the oldest; the tongue-and-groove, the latest. The loose tongue was used on better-class houses from the early 18th Century, till the cheaper tongue-and-groove took over. Boards that were laid without such a joint usually had a thin slip of wood, perhaps an eighth of an inch thick and four inches wide, laid under the joint.

In early floors the handmade nails were meant to be seen, and today we think them quite decorative besides being obvious evidences of antiquity. If the joists are of oak, or the nails are rusted solidly in them, the nails probably cannot be driven in more tightly; they will either bend or break. As a consequence, warped boards cannot be tightened or pulled down with the existing nails. New nails have to be used, and the boards drilled to receive them. If modern finishing nails are used to reinforce the old ones, they should be driven at an angle into the edges of the board, and set so that they cannot be detected. In desperate cases, the boards may need to be dampened on the concave surface, and the edges screwed down. The screws are deeply counterbored,

116

and the holes afterwards sealed with wooden plugs.

In cases where the boards have shrunk so badly that the joints are fully open, the problem is to close the space either from the top or underneath. But permanently tight joints should not be looked for, especially if the house is heated. These floor boards were designed to give and take, and joints are natural even though they do collect dust. If the boards do not have formed joints such as the shiplap, the gap is probably closed on the underside with a thin strip of wood. On occasion the whole floor will be covered with this underflooring. Mention of this recalls a published statement that we encountered some time ago and have heard repeated as authoritative since. This was to the effect that the fine sand sometimes found under the floor boards indicates that the old-timers used sand for insulation! The truth of the matter of course is that living habits two hundred years ago were not so sanitary, and the housewife was forced to sprinkle the floors with sand to simplify cleaning them. The finer sand naturally sifted through to the subfloor!

On a main floor over a cellar, it is often a simple matter to seal the joint from below with thin strips of wood perhaps a quarter of an inch thick and four inches wide. These may be sprung into position between the joists, and held at the center with a pair of small nails. The gap can then be filled from above. This filling needs to be somewhat flexible so that it will accommodate itself to the expansion and contraction of the boards. If the gap is very wide, a long strip of wood can be fastened to the edge of one of the boards with a finishing nail or two—or even glued on. The narrow remaining space may then be filled with a mixture of sawdust and glue, or sawdust and spar varnish, or even with some proprietary filler that is not of the mineral type. For fairly wide gaps we have used papier-mâché (boiled newspaper) soaked in glue. When hard, it can be lightly sanded and stained. But far better than this is the marine caulking compound used for ships' decks. This material never hardens and can be painted over.

Squeaky main-floor boards can often be quietened by driving in a wood shingle between the board and the joist. In floors with a ceiling below, the board must be fastened down tightly. If this pulls it below the level of the next board, it must be taken up, or one end raised sufficiently to allow packing to be inserted, then fastened down tightly, possibly with counterbored screws covered with wood plugs.

Sometimes, of course, boards do have to be replaced, and the problem is how to get them up without damaging other boards. The job is simplified if the board is cracked, and can be pried out by inserting a chisel or bar in the crack. If there is no crack, it may pay to cut the board down the middle with a circular saw—or drill a few holes to make a slot for a hand-saw. If the board is wide and worth salvaging, make the cut near one edge and save the rest.

Replacing such a board with one from the attic may or may not work. Attic boards very often are not jointed, so a joint may need to be cut, and that calls for a board that has a straight edge. These boards are also likely to be thinner or thicker than the regular board, thus complicating the jointing and necessitating packing or planing down the contact areas. If it is decided to turn one or more of the original boards over, it will be found that the undersides are quite rough. This side should therefore be planed, preferably with a round-nose plane so as not to get the surface too flat and characterless. Never use a sander on an old floor; a scraper is much better, but even that needs careful handling. Finally, in choosing any replacement board, see that it is of the same wood, and matches fairly well as to coloring. Stains and finishes are discussed elsewhere.

Patching the Ribs

In restoring the main timbers of a house —whether it is a masonry structure or a wooden one—the procedures are much the same. In the wooden house the timbers most often requiring attention will be the sills and the posts. In the former case, a rotted sill, or a section of one, can usually be replaced by jacking up the wall slightly at that point. First, it is necessary to remove the bottom board and perhaps one row of siding. It is then easy to cut into the bad section. If this occurs at a corner, it may be necessary to cut the sill wood away from the corner post tenon. But if the tenon also is rotted it too can be removed. If it is not rotted, the new sill section will need mortising to receive the tenon and also to form a lap joint with the end sill.

Very often when a sill is rotted at the corner (usually through lack of rainwater drainage), some of the post also will be gone. This necessitates cutting out a section of the post so that a new piece can be scarved to it. Both angles (front and side) of the sill may also need replacing, and these can be scarved into the remaining sections, the joint being held with a wooden pin or an iron bolt.

Wherever a sill has rotted, in both masonry and wooden houses, there is a likelihood that the main floor timbers are affected. Usually the tenons crumble and let the beam end sag. The problem then is to re-attach the timber to the sill. The old method, and still a good one to use, was to pull the beam end up to the sill and hold it there with a pair of heavy iron straps fastened to the sides of the beam and passing through holes drilled in the sill. An alternative is to cut the beam back a couple of feet and add a new length, complete with tenon, by means of a bolted or pegged scarf joint.

In masonry houses there is often trouble where the main timbers rest on, or pass through, the stone or brick wall. The builders of the old stone houses in particular liked plenty of bearing surface for the timbers. As a result, they were inclined to extend the beams almost through the walls. In some cases this necessitated the ends of the timbers being covered by stones that projected beyond the face of the wall. Quite incidentally, it seems, these projecting stones were continued to form a band of masonry at floor level which served as a drip course. This course also, unfortunately, encouraged rainwater to find its way inside and there rot the wood.

Then there are stone houses in which the floor joists pass right through the walls to form supports for the pent roofs. Where these extensions rot at all it seems to be beyond the face of the wall and not inside it —the pent roof keeps out the driving rain and only that which leaks down the face of the wall does the damage. Restoration here calls for a remedy to suit the trouble. If the beams supporting the pent need to be shortened, as often happens, a length may be scarved in. Then the whole is fastened to the stump of the joists in the wall by drilling both and inserting an iron bar. An alternative, which we prefer, is to fasten a separate timber along the outside wall, solidly pegged or spiked to the flush ends of each trimmed joist. The pent-roof timbers are then fastened to this, often without the need for splicing.

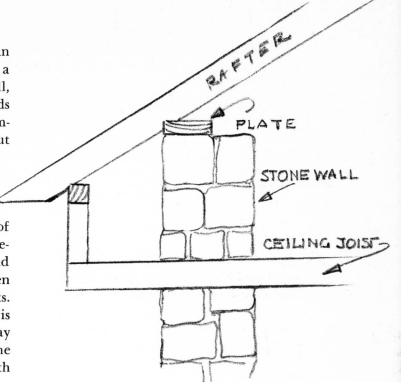

Pent roof framing.

In either case it helps if a good part of the roof weight is taken by the joint between the top ends of the pent rafters and the wall. Usually this is a 3x4-inch wooden plate held to the wall by flat iron brackets. These may need to be tightened. If this is not possible, inverted brackets of wood may be installed over each joist extension, the vertical leg being fastened to the wall with metal spikes.

In both masonry and wooden houses, the heavy timbers such as chimney girts and end girts were often cut away at their centers to support the end of another heavy timber such as a summer beam. This joint materially weakened the chimney girt which was unsupported at the center and therefore sagged or even cracked. In all such cases there is the problem of restoring these timbers without replacing them. In the case of timber ends resting on masonry supports —especially where there are ceilings underneath—scarfing is not wholly satisfactory and usually involves damage to plaster as well as being expensive. There is, in fact, no ideal solution.

On the other hand, if the idea can be tolerated, it is possible to make a permanent repair by using lengths of structural iron. Where a beam enters a wall, a pair of angle irons, let in flush with the wood, are bolted to either side. These form a flat-based extension to the beam that rests on the stonework. The little iron that is exposed can usually be cased in with wood or plaster. An alternative is to remove some of the wall masonry below the beam and insert a projecting stone that will serve as a corbel. Such a corbel can, if necessary, be made a decorative feature. Then there is always the old remedy of inserting a post against the wall under the broken-off end of the beam.

In cases where a beam sags and splits, an invisible repair can be made with a length of T-shaped angle iron. The top of the timber is uncovered, and it is supported in its natural position. Then, with a power saw, a cut is made along the underside of the beam, across the crack or joint. Into this cut is forced the web of the angle-iron which has been drilled through in two places near

119

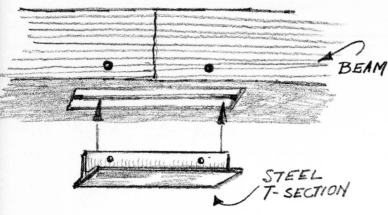

How to patch a beam with steel.

each end. Bolts are inserted through the beam and through these holes. When the nuts—which are counterbored—are tightened, the angle iron rigidly supports the beam. If ordinary iron flitch plates are used to strengthen beams in observable positions, they should be let into the wood the full thickness of the metal so that they are flush with the wood surfaces and therefore not noticeable.

These principles can be applied to the repair of all wooden members of any house, but wherever possible wood should be used for mending wood!

Fixing the Plaster

In small American houses of the 18th Century, interior woodwork gradually gave way to plaster. In the early days it was common practice to whitewash both the woodwork and the plaster as a sanitary measure. As time went on, the layers of whitewash on the plaster grew thicker, and built up an entirely new surface of lime. This gave the old-time interior walls a scaly look of age that it would be hard to duplicate. The one thing it did *not* do was to form trowel patterns on the walls, or even a smooth, glossy surface. These are the two things we have to avoid today in restoring interiors, often

without much co-operation on the part of the plasterer.

Because of this almost universal practice of whitewashing the plaster, it did not matter particularly what color the finished coat of plaster turned out to be. Normally, however, whether the lime used in the plaster was made from sea shells, from coral or limestone, the color was an "off" white. The actual tint depended on the kind of sand used, and the quantity.

In the early days the plaster was applied in at least three coats. The first coat, which formed the key that held the plaster to the lathing, was usually rich in lime and contained considerable cow hair. This was the "scratch" coat. The next layer was the "brown" coat which probably got its name from its color, having about twice as much

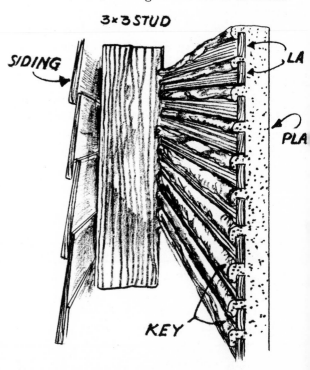

The earliest plastered walls had nothing but air between plaster and siding.

120

sand and plenty of cow hair. The finish coat would have as much lime as the scratch coat but no hair. The proportion of lime could not be increased too much because it would crack on setting. The normal proportions of materials, by volume, would be about 1 lime, 1½ sand for the scratch and finish coats, and 1 lime to 3 sand for the brown coat. The hair (wood fiber is often used nowadays) would average three bushels to the cubic yard of sand for the base coat and one and one-half bushels for the brown coat.

Because of the quality of the materials used, the finished surface would be fairly smooth but by no means glossy. The wall itself would be somewhat wavy, particularly if the studs were not sawn, with a tendency to bulge between the studs. This was due to the fact that the lathing was irregular and inclined to expand and warp slightly when wet—and to stay that way.

The hand-split hemlock or oak lath was used from the earliest Colonial times to the early 19th Century, when sawn pine lath

began to take its place. With the sawn lath, walls became more regular and flatter, and lost a lot of character. In restoration, therefore, it pays to use lathing to match the original. The hand-split laths are easy to

Plank walls offer a poor surface for plaster.

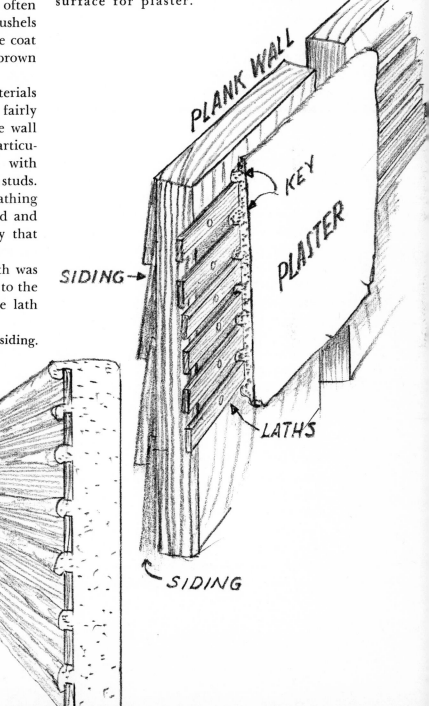

Later houses had sheathing under the siding.

make from a quarter of an inch thick hemlock, split along the grain, first from one end then the other. If it is not possible to get these, the next best thing is to use the sawn lath, bowing it outward slightly when applying it, and leaving the rest to nature and the wet plaster.

Where it is necessary to match a new plastered surface with an old one as to color, an off-white calsomine may be used over both of them, or, in cases of desperation, a thinned interior paint. But much better than either is a proprietary material called *Dramex*. This is a prepared coating that looks like mixed plaster but can be applied with a brush or trowel to any thickness. Even cracked ceilings can be resurfaced with it. As regards the plaster and lathing, using the old materials and the proper proportions of sand and lime will result in a flexible wall that will not crack with the periodic movements of the house frame, and this finish will stay with it.

When plaster has been removed from posts and beams that were originally covered, it should be replaced. Ordinarily, the plaster will have been held to the wood by ax cuts in the surface. These never do form a good key, and must be thoroughly cleaned out of old plaster. Quite often it will be found that the corners of the timbers have strips of wood applied along them to protect the plaster by stopping it short of the angle. If these do not exist, the plastering job may not be too satisfactory. Since any house with this type of finish will not be too old, it may be permissible to encase the timbers instead of replastering them. This will result in a neater, simpler, and permanent job, and an authentic-appearing one provided the casing is formed in the old-

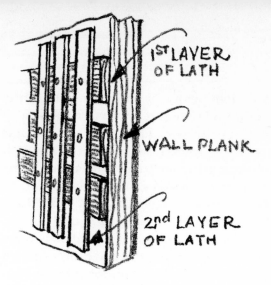

One way of helping plaster adhere to plank walls.

time manner with a beaded, rabbeted joint, and using old wood.

So often in the 19th Century, posts and beams that had been robbed of their casings were plastered in this manner, and the only true restoration is re-casing.

In plastering a plank wall, the old-style method was to nail laths directly to the boards. If the boards were a foot to eighteen inches wide, with rather wavy one-inch gaps between them, the plaster had some chance of keying itself to the wall. Otherwise the plaster could not hook itself to the wood because it could not get behind the laths. Sometimes this space between the boards can be widened with a keyhole saw or chisel. A more drastic cure for loose plank wall plaster is discussed in the remodelling section.

Loose Plaster and Lath

Plaster walls and ceilings may bulge from either of two causes: If the lath comes loose from the studs or ceiling joists, or if the plaster breaks away from the lathing. The latter is the more serious because it is harder to re-attach the plaster to the lath than it is the lath to the joists or studs. On the other hand, it rarely happens that the plaster comes loose over a wide area. Ceilings are more prone to this type of failure due to whipping or looseness of the joists. The laths may break away because they have rotted, or the acids in the oak joists have rusted through the nails.

In the case of ceilings, it is usually necessary to take up a floor board in order to determine what has happened. If the lathing has given way, the whole center area can be gently pushed back into position with one or two boards closely spaced, tied together and supported as a unit with lengths of two-by-four. This will usually bring up most of the surrounding area into position. The parts between the boards and those around them can then be fastened with brass screws into the joists. The screws need to be fitted with galvanized washers, and preferably have a felt washer each side of it. The whole is countersunk into the plaster when the screw hole is drilled through the lath. Don't try to do the job with nails!

With one part secure, the supporting boards can be moved aside slightly, still in firm contact with the ceiling, and the operation continued. The job is finished by patching the screw holes.

If it is the plaster that is loose, the major part of the work will have to be done from above. With the plaster pushed up in position, the old plaster keys are removed from between the laths. This must not be done until the plaster is in position or the keys may fall through and prevent it being raised tight against the laths. The next step is to plaster *over* the laths with a fairly thin plaster mix that will attach itself to the original plaster. Sometimes it is best to use linen rags soaked in plaster to form new keys. Obviously, all of this is a job for a professional plasterer!

The same procedure as used for ceilings can be applied to walls with loose lathing. But if the other side of the wall is not open, the re-attachment of loose plaster calls for other techniques. Loose wall plaster can quite often be held by screws, but the difficulty is to hide the screw heads. Unless the plaster is very thick, countersinking usually won't work. In some rooms a peg board can be installed about five feet up, screwed to the studs, or perhaps a sill-high wainscoting of old pine boards applied over the loose plaster. But not if this is a strictly restoration job. True restoration may call for a re-plaster job using the old-time materials.

How to Fix Bricks

The restoration of brickwork concerns not only walls that have deteriorated but replacement of bricks in chimneys, fireplaces, bake ovens, filled-in windows, steps, and so on. Bricks crack and spall (flake off) from frost and damp, and they also decay. One cause of both these troubles is open joints. Another is continuous dampness. That is why old bricks inside cellars so often turn to powder. The only cure for any of the trouble due to water in the joints is to replace the bad brick and mortar the joints with lime mortar, sometimes with a dash of cement added.

Decay also calls for measures to remove the cause of dampness—possibly by adequate ventilation, or seeing that the roof water does not get into the ground near the house walls. This question is discussed in detail in connection with stone houses, below.

Chimney brickwork too often not only needs restoring but rebuilding. So many of them were built one brick thick, and being attacked by the elements from both sides, quickly rotted out the mortar. Chimneys in that state then need repointing from both inside and out, with all the crumbling mortar first being removed. In many cases it will actually pay to rebuild the entire chimney top above the junction of the flues. Then a good cement mortar can be used, and the joints pointed on the outside with lime mortar.

In restoration, any peanut-sized Victorian chimney mounted on a substantial old-time nest of flues should be torn down and rebuilt. The bricks, of course, should be salvaged for this work, though extra ones will be needed. The soot-stained bricks should have their dirty faces hidden from sight; nothing betrays a rebuilt job more quickly than flue-blackened bricks.

In filling up any wall openings that were not original, the bricks should be carefully matched, and the bonding copied exactly. To get the proper bond, so that no difference will be detected between the old and the new work, a half brick may have to be removed from alternate courses.

One of the commoner difficulties is to find brick of exactly the same size—and age—as the originals; another is to match the color. Luckily, in many instances the old bricks varied widely in color—perhaps from salmon pink to clay brown—even in the same wall. This gives the restorer some latitude, but there is still the matter of texture to be considered. This means using pretty near the same quality of brick throughout—not mixing very crudely made ones with others that are perfectly straight and square.

Where brick fireplaces have to be rebuilt, the original dimensions should be kept, and the courses over the fireplace opening always laid flat. And where a mantel or panelling surrounds the opening, no more than two, or perhaps three, courses of bricks should be exposed, or more than half to two-thirds of a brick at the sides.

Both internal and outdoor bake ovens can be repaired by following the old method of construction described earlier. If only one brick has fallen out, it can be replaced from the inside by wetting the hole, using a stiff lime mortar, and propping the brick in position till the mortar has thoroughly set—probably several days. Where external bake ovens have been knocked off and the opening bricked up, the only serious problem may be installing a new supporting

HEARTH BRICK PATTERN

stone or timber brackets. So often the original stone base was broken off flush with the wall. The problem then is to remove the remaining piece of stone and replace it with a complete one. This calls for patience rather than skill. The oven is rebuilt of brick by the sand method. If the complete oven was originally of brick it will have been two bricks thick, and almost always, where exposed to the weather, given a good, smooth coating of stucco. If the house walls are of stone, the outer covering of the oven also may have been of stone—perhaps stuccoed, perhaps not. If the original oven base was supported by timbers, the new ones will have to go into the wall the full depth of the old timbers and be securely mortared in place. After the mortar is set hard, the stone slab can be mounted on them. Some such ovens were built on two-inch oak planks laid over the timbers. Sources of the old bricks from which the oven can be made are discussed later, in connection with Reproductions.

Salvaging Materials

As a rule, the old materials are more easily salvaged than bought—and cost less that way. And since the purpose of restoration, either as an end in itself or as a part of remodeling, is to preserve as much of the original as possible, the extra work involved is more than justified.

No old board should be thrown away, regardless of how small it is. A scrap of one-inch old pine no more than ten by twenty may make a replacement panel for a cupboard door; that foot-long strip of molding may replace a damaged section somewhere else.

Save all the nails you can, even if they have an inch of the point broken off. If they won't hold down a thick board, they will still serve in place of screws for an old latch. Some good sawn planks were used for plank walls. Even if they seem rough, and have plaster lath nailed to them, they will look quite different after being planed down—especially if the plane has a slightly rounded iron!

Restoring Stone Structures

In stone houses with very thick walls— say two feet or over—the two outer surfaces may be built of moderate-sized stone with a fairly loose filling between them. If frost gets into the wall, or the mortar decays, either one or both sides may bulge, and eventually collapse.

Localized bulges can sometimes be cured by forcing the stones back into position with the help of a suitable jack and something solid to rest it against, then running cement grout into the wall interior through a hole in a higher joint. In other cases, where there has been some displacement inside the wall, the stones may have to be removed and reset in cement, then pointed in lime mortar to maintain the old appearance.

Ordinarily in the case of most house walls there will be adequate bonding so that the walls cannot bulge, though they may settle and crack. Repairs to such walls therefore largely consist of replacing stones, or of filling gaps with mortar. In all such cases the original mortar should be copied as closely as possible. This usually means using three or four parts of local sand to one part of lime—the sand being as coarse, or as fine, as the original, and the same color. The original joints should be copied exactly. Heavy masonry walls that have cracked or moved will, of course, call for the services of a competent mason.

Wet Walls

Most old-time masonry houses need insulating against dampness. The majority of these houses today have a plaster finish applied directly to the inside surface of their exterior walls and this has no insulating value. The livability of such a house depends on the degree of dampness of the walls which usually are cold enough to condense any excess moisture in the interior air. Keeping the walls dry, therefore, is a problem not easily solved, short of the drastic measure discussed in the *Remodelling* section.

In combating dampness, the logical approach is first to make sure that the walls are not absorbing moisture from wet ground. If the ground is wet, there may be need for the asphalting of the foundation walls below grade, or even laying a tile drain to carry off water in the ground. A first essential, however, is to see that rainwater is not allowed to soak into the ground close to the foundation walls. This may be done by installing gutters, or by laying flagstones against the foundation to drain off the roof water. Merely grading the earth away from the house may do the trick in some cases.

Stucco helps to keep the water from getting into the masonry joints, and adds to the life of stonework generally. In no case should the stucco be removed unless it is certainly a recent addition. Properly finished, and perhaps whitened, it can determine the whole architectural value of the façade. A misguided craze for crudity, or a mistaken belief that the stucco is modern, has resulted in the spoiling of many a stone house. Ordinarily, stucco cannot be removed without pulling some of the mortar out of the joints. A thorough pointing job, therefore, will be needed if the house is restored by uncovering the masonry. Never remove the stucco without first making certain that the stone underneath it is not of a porous kind. The stucco was probably put on for a purpose that is just as valid today!

Any old house that has an original or very early plaster or stucco coating on the outside should have that coating properly restored both because of appearance and as an aid to keeping the walls dry and sound. The whole area should be thoroughly examined for cracks or broken-out patches, especially around windows and doors and drip-courses, and the upper edges of pent roofs. All cracks and openings or thin spots need to be filled and sealed. When properly patched, the whole area can be made weatherproof by painting with a cement paint or a proprietary sealer called *Super Bondex* that will preserve the original color of the stucco. A good deal of the old stucco was actually whitewashed, and a white finish is one of the best—and likely to be most authentic—for stucco masonry houses.

Naked stone, as well as brick, calls first for attention to the joints. Careful repointing is a necessity, with the mortar firmly smoothed as soon as it begins to harden so that no ledges are left to hold water. Split stones can have the crack filled with mortar, but soft, porous ones may need replacing. If the joints are very bad, it may be better to partially fill them with cement mortar and finish pointing with lime mortar so as not to spoil the appearance. A little Portland cement can often be added to the mortar without changing the color appreciably, but with red sandstone an excess of lime will be needed to make the joints dead white.

If any large area of stones has to be replaced, the stones and mortar may need coloring slightly to match the surrounding materials. We are told that a mushy mixture of clay and cow dung well rubbed in works well, but the idea is not enticing. A coating of local mud, removed when dry with a bristle brush would probably serve as well.

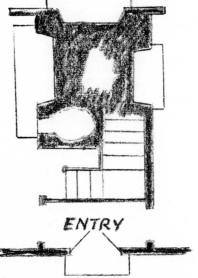

ENTRY

Blocked off entry and rear stair alongside the bake oven.

Restoration Examples

The complete restoration of any house is rarely undertaken except for museum or historical organization purposes. On the other hand the kinds and conditions of antique houses that are available today very often do need strict restoration of some important part of the structure. In this respect, the kind of thing the new owner is likely to run into can very well be illustrated by instances from our records.

The first of these concerns a 1776, one and a half story center-chimney house that had its original staircase replaced. This was obvious because the new stair was of new oak with seven-inch risers in place of the nine-inch risers common to this type of house. In addition, the stair made a ninety-degree turn at the bottom, leaving a three-foot space between it and the chimney. The handrail and stringer moldings were of clearly modern patterns.

These facts impelled us to look for further evidence, and this we discovered in the patches of ceiling plaster and marks on the floor boards indicating that a partition had extended from the chimney to the entry and returned parallel with the front house wall to form part of the entry. This guess was further confirmed by the fact that the entry floor was quite worn at the place where the stair would normally start.

In any case the new stair would have to be removed and a new one built of old wood in the antique manner to replace it. On taking out the stair it was at once seen that a much steeper stair had run down the right-hand wall separating it from the right-hand room.

The position of the old open string was clearly defined by the dust on the studs. Above, it could be seen where the plaster had been chopped away to accommodate the modern closed stringer. A chalk line from the upper floor to the entry floor indicated the angle of the stair to be made, from which it was easy to work out the dimensions of the treads and risers.

The new stringers were cut out of two-inch planks that had once been part of a two-story plank wall. The treads and risers were made of one-inch pine as old as the house. And of course old nails were used.

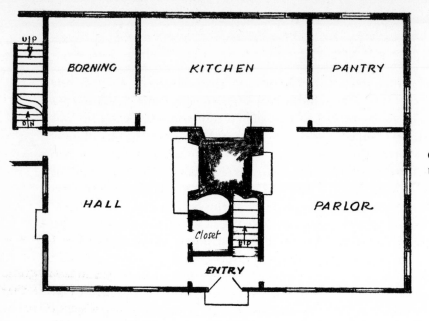

BORNING   KITCHEN   PANTRY

UP

DN

HALL

Closet

PARLOR

UP

ENTRY

Old stair rising from the entry across the back of the parlor fireplace.

The risers came down behind the treads, where they were nailed through into the back edges of the treads with four hand-made nails apiece.

The only crisis came when it was discovered that the new left-hand stringer would have to be cut away slightly so as not to cut into the top of the bake oven. The carpenter would have preferred to chop away some of the bricks! In these old stairs which have no closed stringer to form a sort of baseboard at the ends of each step, the plaster actually comes down to the step. Due to the change in the angle of the steps, there was a triangular strip growing wider toward the bottom that had to be lathed and plastered.

What we now had was a straight run of stairs going up from the entry, across the back of the chimney shoulder. The shoulder was formed by masonry extending to the right-hand room wall so as to accommodate a fireplace. To the left of the stair was a rectangular space formerly occupied by the bottom three steps of the new stair. In this space, the floor boards ran at right angles to the room floorboards—that is, parallel with the front wall. At the junction of

the two sets of boards were the nail marks of an old partition. This was verified by scraping off a little of the ceiling plaster along this line from the chimney face to the house front wall. This plaster was white all through and quite different from the sandy-brown old plaster around it. Evidently the original plaster had been applied after the partition was in place—a common practice in the early days. In the remodelling, the unplastered strip had been filled in with modern patching plaster. The rest was a matter of logic. These entries were always shut off from the room by a door. The space next to the chimney most certainly was cut off to form a closet.

This partition was therefore installed with two adjoining doors. At the same time the partitions to enclose the stair and to separate the entry from the closet were installed. These were made of feather-edge sheathing on the entry side—to match that elsewhere in the house—and wide, lap-jointed boards to enclose the stair. The final job was to add a door at the foot of the stair—a necessity in the old days if a nuisance today.

In striking contrast to this job was a

128

smaller restoration that even the owner was not aware needed doing. The interior of this museum-like house seemed perfect. Most of it was late 17th Century, the rooms being divided by featheredged boarding and an occasional section of beautiful raised panelling.

With these dark interiors it is not always possible to see details, and it was not until we checked the room layout that something seemed amiss. In these smaller old houses very little space was wasted, particularly on passageways. The house was a Southern Colonial of masonry with end chimneys, but the main entrance was directly into the kitchen, five feet from one gable—a very early type of plan. This old kitchen extended from front to back of the house. To the right of this was a large front room with its own fireplace in one corner. Back-to-back with that fireplace was a smaller one in the next room.

It was this small back room that excited our interest because it was closed off with a feather-edged board partition that formed a passageway leading from the front room to the rear house door. In this passageway were the stairs to the second floor. Such an urge for privacy is unusual in these small houses, and we wanted to know why. The woodwork was exquisite and there was so much of it. We put the measured plan down on paper, and at once began to see what might have happened.

The house must originally have had three rooms, with the stair and back door in one of them. The small room had evidently been closed off later, though the fact was not immediately obvious. The next thing was to make a detailed examination of the suspected partition, and our suspicion was justified. What told the story was that in one corner near the ceiling on the passage side, we found the panels had lost their top rail. This evidently had been sawed off to make it fit, cutting away the tapered edges of the panels themselves. The panels were not fastened to the ceiling in any way.

Restoration here consisted merely of removing the partitions to throw the passage into the two rooms. It was then seen that the stair was actually a decorative feature of one of them. Its beautiful panelling had not been visible in the narrow passageway.

As a final example, not only of the detective work necessary in planning authentic restorations, but also as a warning against too much enthusiasm in the process, here is an instance of "restoration" actually ruining an ancient house.

This house was built of stone around 1700. Originally it had been a nice, two-story, end-chimney farmhouse with a very steep roof and small, leaded casement windows and a massive beehive oven in the basement. Through the centuries it had first acquired larger windows of the sash type, including lights to the basement whose ceiling was two feet above ground level.

In the late 18th Century the house had been stuccoed. In the 19th Century the stucco was removed and the beautifully laid ledge stone was painted brown to match the Victorian additions in wood. Some of the wood panelling over the interior walls had been removed and the walls plastered. One of the interior panelled partitions had been replaced by a plastered wall. The original tall chimneys had been bobbed three feet. The old staircase was in bad condition and the main beams—twenty-four feet long—were rotted. In the basement the original clay floor had apparently been flagged early in its history, then concreted over.

Some years ago the house once more came into possession of descendants of the original owner, and a full restoration was decided upon. While the Victorian additions were being lopped off, old documents were being studied to determine exactly how the old house had looked—and there was plenty of detailed information both in descriptions and drawings. The proud descendants of the builder decided to honor him by restoring the house to its original state as of the year 1700!

As it turned out, that was an unfortunate decision because so little of the original structure—except the main walls—was left. The first set-back came when the exterior walls were sandblasted to remove the paint. The shell of the house now looked as though it had been built yesterday. This illusion was heightened when the brick chimneys were restored. Instead of using old brick, and retaining as much of the old chimneys as possible, both were taken down to ridge height and rebuilt in modern hard-faced brick. In three of the brick were stamped the builder's initials and the date of erection, the lettering carefully painted black. How easy it would have been to make those bricks in the old-time way, and incise the letters and figures in the antique style!

Going back to 1700 meant reproducing the old casements and diamond calmes. The result was obviously modern leaded glass which the new frames were not cut to fit exactly. Half-inch pieces of glass were needed to fill in. The old door was reproduced in modern wood, sawn and planed in the modern manner, and held together with today's reproductions of old nails. And so it went!

The huge beams could not be replaced, so steel girders were boarded over to represent them, the lower corners carefully chamfered right into the plaster! The feather-edged board partitions were carefully duplicated; random pieces of flagstone were laid in the basement, and everything done to duplicate the old materials with modern ones. Outside, all the woodwork was daubed with the old-time red paint made in the old-time way of old-time materials. But no one would ever know that!

What started out as a restoration was largely a reproduction that would have been more convincing if a later date had been chosen—a date that would have left more of the house to be salvaged. From this sad example of misguided "restoration" it is quite clear that to be satisfying, any restoring must have as its basis a reasonable amount of the original structure in its natural condition—and recognizable for what it is. And the rest of the work done to it—the supplying of the deficiencies—must be done with old materials, worked in the old-time way with the tools of that day. Anything less will be a constant, jarring reminder of what has been lost instead of what is left!

Chapter VII

Remodelling vs Remuddling

THE remodelling of any house is in many ways a much simpler job than restoration. In remodelling you adapt the house to your special needs while striving to retain the old features that are left and recapture in some degree the old-time atmosphere. Normally, you have a great deal of latitude in what you can do, because any house suitable for remodelling has probably had many things done to it in the past that would be improved by any change at all. The important thing, however, is to proceed as you would in restoration as far as possible—destroying nothing old and restoring rather than replacing what must be salvaged or rebuilt. Every old item saved adds that much more authentic atmosphere to the finished job.

How far can you go beyond this depends for one thing upon how much the house is to be used. If it is to be lived in the year round it will naturally need a few things done to it that mere summer residence does not demand. For one thing, the fireplaces will be used, and that calls for careful investigation of the flues. The old chimneys are almost always leaky, especially above the attic floor. Any fireplace that has been closed off can also be a hazard because it may have burnable material accumulated in it which can be ignited by a spark from another fireplace or from burning soot. Another thing to look for is a "stuffed chimney"—a flue packed with paper or rags to keep out the draft.

The first thing to be done, therefore, is to have the flues thoroughly cleaned. The stack should be looked over for cracks and leaky or open joints—often indicated by tar leaks on the outside. Where possible, it should be inspected on the inside, at least as far down as the junction of the separate flues. It can also be examined visually upward from each fireplace. If the visible parts are obviously in bad shape, the whole chimney may be suspected, and steps should be taken to see that it is made sound. There are several ways of doing this, but one sure method is to line all usable flues with a special metal pipe made for the purpose. This lining is let down from the top till it rests on a pair of metal bars let into the fireplace throat. It is then sealed top and bottom with mortar. Being coated with ceramic, this pipe will last indefinitely.

Sometimes earthenware flue tile can be used, but making good joints in irregular flues is difficult. A leaky chimney top above the flue junction usually needs to be rebuilt, though it may be repointed with cement mortar, or even stuccoed to make it weatherproof, especially if it is to be repainted. All of these things need to be considered if a furnace is to be put in and use one of the flues.

Any heating system at all will call for a chimney, or at least a flue. Many owners are content to sacrifice a fireplace to the furnace so that its flue may be used, but that is not altogether a happy solution. If the house has a leanto, ell, or extension (old or new), it is sometimes possible to confine a heating plant of the forced circulation type (whether of air or water) to that area and provide it with a separate chimney. This can be a simple metal flue extending through the roof at a point where it will be most inconspicuous. Such a chimney does not need to extend above the height of the main roof because it is more in the nature of an exhaust vent and does not need to provide a draft. It should, of course, be kept well away from any window.

As a last resort, a chimney of brick with a tile lining can be built against the house gable wall, extending a couple of feet above the roof, preferably on the back slope. If the lower part is of masonry to match the gable, or painted the same color as the house if it is of wood, and then painted black or dark gray above the roof, it will be hardly noticeable.

Heating Systems

In installing any heating system in an antique house, the first consideration should be its effect on the structure. The house timbers and woodwork should not be subjected to greater extremes of heat than necessary. With the possibility of shrinking and warping always present, the gentler the heat and the more even the circulation, the less likelihood of trouble. The system that best fills these conditions therefore is forced-circulation hot water, and the worst is the hot-air floor furnace. Almost as good as forced hot-water is the circulated warm-air system, but this has other drawbacks. The large ducts, vents, and return grilles cut up the floors and walls, and limit the use of a low-ceilinged cellar. From the housekeeper's point of view, there is always the factor of moving air through the rooms, which keeps the dust stirred up.

The water systems demand only small holes cut in the floors and ceilings, and second floors can be heated without large ducts climbing the walls; half-inch copper tubing or one and a half-inch pipes are easier to conceal. Contrariwise, the warm-air outlets do not take up room or interfere with the placing of furniture, as do the radiators and convectors. Except, perhaps, in the case of plank walls! For houses not occupied the year-round the warm-air system has the advantage that it can be shut off and turned on without having to drain the system or call in a plumber. In choosing a heating system, therefore, one should balance possible damage to the structure against convenience. After which, strict attention should be paid to the manner of installation. This will become obvious as we go into the matter of that other necessary evil—plumbing.

Installing Bathrooms

Adequate plumbing is, of course, a basic essential in adapting any house to modern living. In an antique house, unfortunately, it affords the plumber a number of opportunities of saving time and effort at the expense of the structure. In installing a bathroom, for example, it is necessary to run a four-inch cast-iron pipe to the sewer or septic tank, and also to run that same pipe up through the roof as a vent (though it may be reduced in diameter at the top). The normal place for a bathroom is against an outside wall, and that is where the pipe usually goes. Only after the hole is cut in the downstairs bathroom floor does the plumber discover that the sill projects inwards beyond the wall. This means that part of the sill must be cut away. When he tries to run the pipe up through the ceiling he similarly finds that the girt interferes, and more surgery is necessary.

In the second-floor bathroom the washbowl may be on an inner wall, so that the waste pipe has to run under the floor to the soil pipe. To get the necessary fall to the pipe, either parts of the joists have to be cut away or the pipe must go beneath the downstairs ceiling. And usually it is the joists that get cut. Notching the joists is sometimes unavoidable, but they can be strengthened either by bridging over the cut or by stiffening the sides.

The important thing is to plan the layout most carefully before even taking up a board or drilling a hole. If a large pipe must run from floor to ceiling, away from sill and girt, it can always be boxed-in to look like a post. It can also be insulated against noise.

In deciding upon a bathroom location, the positioning of the water and drain pipes should first be considered. If there is a water supply to an existing kitchen, the bathroom should be either over or alongside it. And one bathroom over another will save a great deal of expense besides limiting the necessary butchering of the house.

Whenever an old house has plumbing installed for the first time, it is as well to look into the advantages, in that area, of lightning rods. It is thought that bringing metal pipes into the house, especially to second-floor bathrooms, may add to the danger since these are metallic conductors, well grounded, that act as a partially concealed rod. Though the lightning follows the pipe to the ground it can do a lot of damage on the way. The fact that the house has stood intact for two hundred years immune to lightning is therefore no guarantee that it will continue to do so. *Verbum sat sapienti!*

Insulation

Insulating a wooden house introduces quite a different set of problems to those of insulating a masonry house and they therefore need to be considered separately. Ordinarily, the insulation of an antique frame house consists of removing some of the outer covering, drilling a three-inch round hole in the sheathing (if any) and blowing the loose, or pellet-form, insulating material into the spaces between the studs, over and under the braces. If the walls are of plank instead of studs this obviously cannot be done, and other means have to be adopted.

One trouble with simply filling the walls is that this sometimes causes the paint to peel off the siding. This is due to warm, moisture-laden air passing outward through the plaster and being condensed when it strikes the cold, inside surface of the siding.

When a *new* wall is insulated, roll insulation is used which incorporates a vapor barrier that stops this action. In the old

133

wall, however, the vapor can only be stopped before it passes through the plaster. This means that the plaster must be painted with some air-tight material, such as a couple of coats of aluminum paint, or sheets of paper-backed aluminum foil that can be hidden under paint.

One way of dealing with the plank wall is to add another surface to its interior face, with insulation of some sort sandwiched in between. This can take the form of insulating board with wooden sheathing as the interior finish. Simpler, though perhaps no cheaper, would be a lining of the walls with plaster board that has an aluminum foil surface, and finishing with plaster. In either case it would be necessary to extend the window and door trim to take in the extra thickness. A much better solution, as a rule, is to remove the siding and install insulating sheathing. The siding is re-installed over the sheathing, and molding applied to window and door trim to bring it level.

In the case of a roof, the usual procedure is to fill the spaces between the attic floor joists with loose insulating material. Roll-type insulation usually cannot be used because of the non-standard spacing of the joists and their irregular surfaces. Also, if the attic is floored it would be quite expensive to install. If the attic itself is to be kept cool, insulation must go between the rafters. Enclosing the spaces and using loose fill will not serve because there must be an air space between the top of the insulation and the underside of the roofing material. Reflective insulation of aluminum foil is excellent, if you can find any wide enough, but it needs protection. Hardboard coated with aluminum might serve but usually the rafters are so irregular that the board cannot be nailed tightly to more than two of

them. If the rafters *can* be boarded in (or between), batt insulation can be used, cut and laid horizontally. But remember, wood shingles will not last very long unless air can get to them and they dry quickly underneath.

Sound-proofing follows similar lines, though interior walls and casings around pipes can be filled with sawdust. Where new partitions are installed, or a single-thickness board partition is doubled, the modern system of staggered studs can be adopted. This consists of attaching one wall to each alternate stud; the other wall to the remaining studs. Blanket insulation passes through the clearance spaces between studs and walls.

Insulating Masonry Walls

The only reliable method of making sure the rooms in masonry houses will be dry and warm is to install a vapor-proof wall inside the original one. First the wall— whether bare stone, brick, or plaster—can be sealed with a bituminous compound painted on. The two-inch by two-inch lathing strips are nailed to the wall to carry the laths. Since the lathingstrips are only one and three-fourths of an inch thick, there will not be much air space between the wall and the new plaster forced between the laths. But what there is will constitute fair insulation. This method unfortunately does involve re-installing the door and window trim, the baseboards, the cornices, if any, plus filling the gaps left around the windows and doors. It also sadly detracts from the old-time appearance of the walls. Don't do it unless you have to!

Methods of curing dampness in masonry walls were discussed in the *Restoration* section.

Power and Light

Electrical work on the old house may consist of anything from installing additional outlets to complete wiring. Starting outside the house, the neatest—and safest—method of getting power into the house is by underground conduit. It costs more but it does not detract from the old-time air. In these days of multiple, heavy-duty appliances—from washers to air-conditioning systems—a three-wire service rated at thirty amperes should be the minimum.

If all of the walls are hollow (and not full of insulation) there will be no problem in carrying wiring to outlets and fixtures in the standard manner with BX cable. With solid walls, however, surface wiring will have to be used. This need cause no concern, for with the neat modern systems the conduits will scarcely be noticeable. The casings can be run up corners and through closets, and you can have all the outlets you want by running outlet strips along the top of the baseboards which they can be painted to match.

What does need to be guarded against is the tendency for electricians to knock over-large holes in plaster and drape BX over attic floors, besides drilling through ceiling joists. An arrangement should be made to have some competent person take up attic and other floor boards and re-lay them without damage after the wiring is completed.

One appliance that may cause some trouble is the kitchen exhaust fan. This usually calls for an outlet at ceiling level, perhaps under the stove hood. The fan switch may be of the drop-cord type, or wired into a cabinet alongside the stove. The fan duct can sometimes be installed between the ceiling joists without tearing down the plaster. But if the joists run in the opposite direction, the duct will have to be below the ceiling. In such a case it may be made no larger than the exterior wall outlet provided by the fan maker. Fastened up in a corner of the ceiling, and painted to match the adjoining surfaces, it should be unobtrusive. Ducts that are of necessity large and unavoidably conspicuous are often best exaggerated by turning them into a decorative feature. One of our most successful fan ducts was made wholly of gleaming copper that gave the old-pine kitchen a needed "lift."

Some Remodelling Examples

At this point it may be both interesting and instructive to study a couple of actual remodellings, each of which offered individual problems—as most remodellings do.

The first of these was an old New-England farmhouse that was originally a central-chimney, one and a half story, braced-frame type built in 1805—though one would never guess it at first glance. Deep, dark porches shaded the entire front of the house, including the kitchen extension. The ground floor had been enlarged at the rear by adding a single-story leanto that was six feet short of making it a "saltbox." The original clapboards had been shingled over, and all blinds removed. The lower sash in all windows had been replaced with single lights. Altogether, it was a somber-looking mess despite beautiful trees, neat lawn, and privet hedge. (Fig. 126.) We tackled it without knowing exactly what we would find.

The first anachronism to be abolished was, of course, the porch—a comparatively simple job even though the rafters were firmly nailed to the house studs. (Sometimes they rest on a 2 x 4 nailed over

KITCHEN

PANTRY

BREAKFAST

KEEPING

BORNING

UP DOWN

CLOSET

PARLOR

UP DOWN

BEDROOM

ENTRY

DORMER

Roof

BEDROOM

STORAGE

BEDROOM

DOWN

UP

CL

CL

BEDROOM

CL

BEDROOM

DOWN

KITCHEN

BATH

KEEPING

BORNING

DINING

UP DOWN

PARLOR

ENTRY

FUNERAL DOOR

ELL ROOF

BATH

DOWN

STORAGE

BEDROOM

BEDROOM

STORAGE

DOWN

LANDING

STORAGE

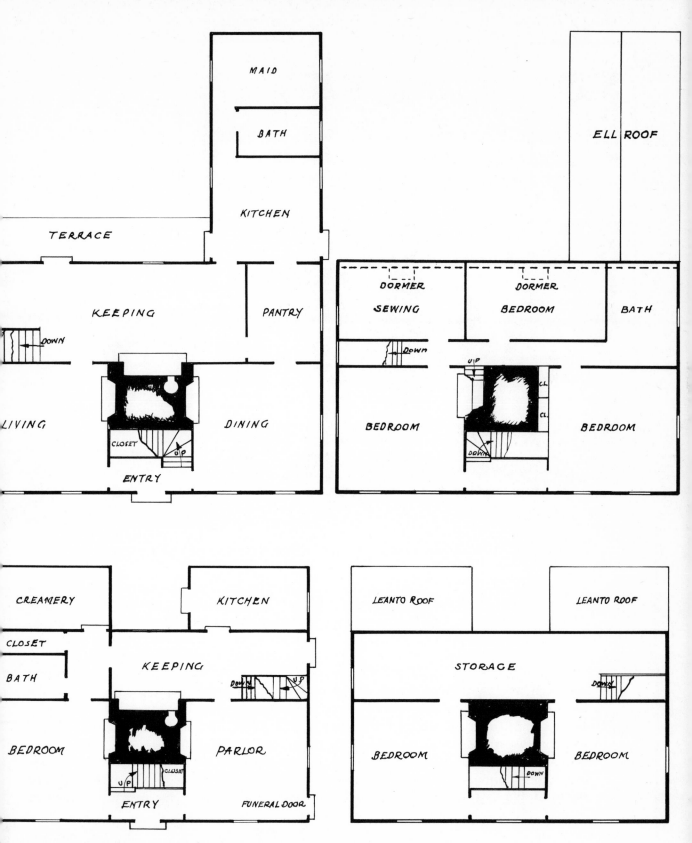

MAID

BATH

ELL ROOF

KITCHEN

TERRACE

KEEPING

PANTRY

DORMER

SEWING

DORMER

BEDROOM

BATH

DOWN

DOWN

UP

CL.

CL.

LIVING

CLOSET

UP

DINING

BEDROOM

DOWN

BEDROOM

ENTRY

CREAMERY

KITCHEN

LEANTO ROOF

LEANTO ROOF

CLOSET

BATH

KEEPING

DOWN

UP

STORAGE

DOWN

BEDROOM

UP

CLOSET

PARLOR

BEDROOM

DOWN

BEDROOM

ENTRY

FUNERAL DOOR

Leanto house floor plans need not be so stereo-
typed as believed. Here we have four examples
of different arrangements, upstairs and down.

An old New England farmhouse—this is what we had to work with. Fig. 126.

the siding!) As the front rail and pillars crashed to the ground amid cries of "T-i-i-m-m-b-b-e-e-r-r!" from grinning onlookers, and clouds of seventy-year-old dust, we began to see what we had.

In building the porch, the house door had been severely bobbed. Problem Number One: what to do with the doorway? Before that could be decided we made another discovery. With the porch roof gone, the wide, blank space over the door looked suspicious. Removing a few shingles disclosed the fact that there had at one time been a window there. The opening had been boarded over and the shingles nailed to the boards. What to do about that? Here were two interrelated problems that circumstances helped us solve. Investigation on the second floor revealed that a partition had been built down the center of the old window space so as to form two bedroom closets. These we needed to keep, so the partition must remain. Then there was the front door. With no window above it, the logical way of breaking up the blank space was to make the doorway higher. A

The extension in particular called for major surgery—inside and out.

triangular pediment took care of that.

Another immediate decision to be made was whether or not to strip off the siding shingles. These had been applied in the late 1800s. To keep them from projecting beyond the windows, moldings had been applied to the trim. That was why we suspected something under the shingles in the first place. Now, though we would have preferred white clapboards to the red-brown shingles, to change back would have been tremendously costly. Removing a few shingles at the rear, we had discovered that

the old siding was in bad shape, and nailing the shingles directly over them had not improved matters. The shingles, therefore, remained.

The next urgent matter was the extension porch. It only took a superficial examination to disclose that this, too, was a later addition; everything was nailed over the original structure with cut nails. So that, too, must come off. The front wall of this extension accommodated both a door and a window. The same room had a door to the back porch, and two interior doors.

Fig. 127a.

The front one we could well do without. This extension room was the old kitchen, but it was about to become a study, and more light would be required; *ergo,* more window space was needed. Therefore the small original window was removed, and a six-foot-wide small-paned fixed sash was installed. This was made into a square bay window by setting it forward on brackets, thus providing a wide window bottom inside, and adding to the apparent width of the room. As the photo shows (Fig. 127a), the proportions of the window in comparison with the size of the building detracted very little from the old-time "feel" of the façade. One other point that had to be settled in connection with this window was its relation to the floor and eaves lines. As is so often the case, this extension sagged noticeably, and the floor sloped toward the free end. The normal tendency in such a case would be to set the window parallel with the floor. On the other hand, this serves to exaggerate, and therefore draw attention to, the sag. Setting the window vertical offset the sag somewhat, as the

140

The finished job, ready for landscaping and the interior work.

photo shows, and actually improved the appearance.

Remodelling the Interior

The interior remodelling called for a re-arrangement of the rooms and the addition of a downstairs washroom. Examination of the rooms showed what the plan did not reveal—that the old kitchen would make a highly desirable living room or study. Being in the wing, it was more or less isolated from the rest of the house; it was large, and gave access to a rear porch; it had a large fireplace, and the front overlooked a delightful view.

A study of the plan, and checking of the water and drain systems, showed us that the old dining room could very well become the kitchen, while the pantry between dining room and kitchen could be turned into a washroom with no plumbing difficulties. A comparison of the before-and-after plans will show that little structural alteration was needed, and considerable floor space—formerly occupied by a passage—was salvaged.

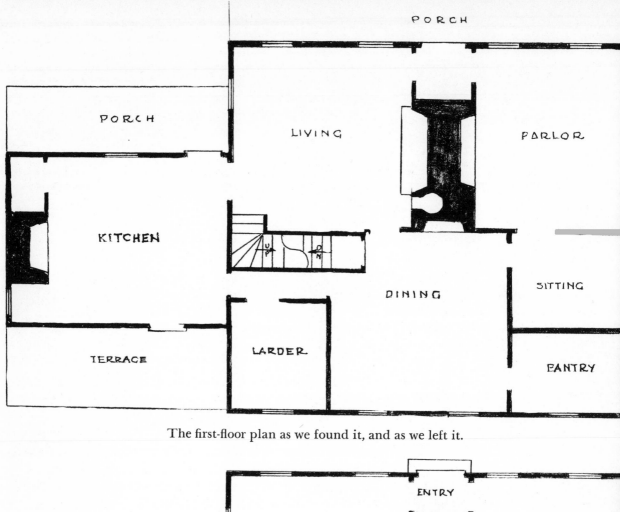

PORCH

PORCH

LIVING

PARLOR

KITCHEN

UP

DN

DINING

SITTING

TERRACE

LARDER

PANTRY

The first-floor plan as we found it, and as we left it.

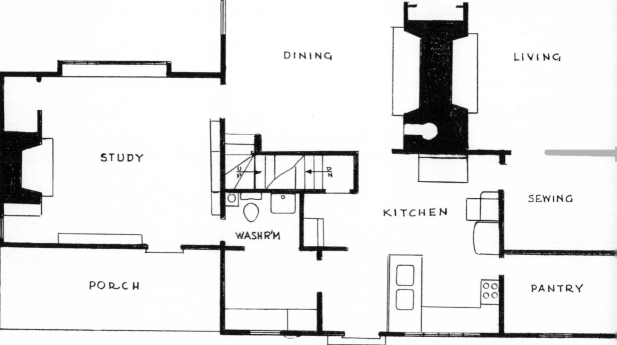

ENTRY

DINING

LIVING

STUDY

UP

DN

KITCHEN

SEWING

WASHR'M

PORCH

PANTRY

Kitchen into Study

Apart from the installation of the large window mentioned earlier, the room remodelling was largely one of salvage. At first glance the room was a Victorian horror. A white enamel and cast-iron coal stove balanced a galvanized hot-water tank on its hip. Water pipes traversed the ceiling and wall to connect with a high-backed white enamel sink. Several layers of linoleum in various stages of dissolution covered the floor, while iron sheets and painted boards hid the fireplace whose presence was betrayed by a seven-foot mantel. Little planning could be done till the fireplace stood revealed. The stove was therefore the first thing to go.

The brick fireplace proved to have a five-foot opening but no bake oven. The back hearth had sagged several inches below the floor level, and the hearthstone was gone. Above the mantel, a shallow cupboard had lost its door and a hole had been cut through the back for a stove pipe.

Salvage of the fireplace started with an inspection of its foundations. Fortunately, a hatchway in the end wall gave access below the floor. Here it was found that the hearth foundations were slabs of stone piled up without mortar. Some of them had slipped out of place, letting the back hearth down. These same stones had supported the rear of the hearthstone, the front edge resting on a floor joist. When the stone was removed, the hearth had been boarded over.

The whole thing was restored by building up the foundation, setting the stones in cement. Since the recommended height of a five-foot fireplace opening is thirty-nine inches, and this was forty-two inches, it was decided to raise the hearth one brick, and probably cure a smoky chimney. The foundation was therefore extended to take in the area of the old hearthstone, and the whole built up to the floor level. On top of that, the finished hearth was built of old brick set on edge. This brick hearth was held in place by a 2 x 4 frame with chamfered edges, nailed to the wood floor. The job was completed by having the mason set in a damper of the ring-operating type.

The back panel of the doorless cupboard over the fireplace could not be replaced without tearing out the whole frame. It was therefore decided to cover the back with another board of old pine. This was carefully fitted and held by invisible finishing nails. At the same time, two shelves were fitted and the whole thing painted to match the rest of the trim.

Because of the bad condition of the lower part of the walls, and to provide a finish below the new big window, a dado of wide horizontal boards was installed right around the room. This tied together the fireplace, built-in bookcases, door frames and so on, and the horizontal line helped make the room seem larger.

The wide floor boards were quite rough, particularly in front of the fireplace where firewood had apparently been chopped. The bad place was smoothed a little by planing because sanding such a floor takes away all its character. The grease- and dirt-stained floor boards were then scrubbed and finally painted a rich dark antique red.

The cracked and battered ceiling from which the pipe hangers had been removed was skimmed over with white Dramex applied with a brush to get the old-time rough-plaster finish. The upper parts of the walls above the dado were papered with a docu-

mentary print to heighten the old-time air. With the woodwork a medium Williamsburg green, the paper selected had a rich red background and diamond pattern in green with touches of yellow and white.

THE STAIRS

A small but important improvement to the living room (which later became the dining room) was the enclosing of the stairs to elbow height. This rail-less stair, ascending from the living room, was neither decorative nor safe. Long ago the rail had been removed, doubtless with the idea of permitting furniture to be jockeyed up and down the stairs, and never replaced.

The hopeless looking kitchen seen here, became this comfortable study.

144

It was obvious that with a seven foot six inch ceiling and a narrow stair, there would always be difficulty in maneuvering dressers and beds up and down. Detailed examination of the trim revealed that the stair had once been entirely enclosed, with a door at the bottom. That would have been an ideal arrangement in some respects. It would give the living room added wall space, which it needed with its three doors and three windows. The door would have eliminated drafts, but the stair would have been dark, and unnavigable with anything larger than a suitcase. A compromise was therefore decided upon.

We enclosed the stair to within six inches

Remodeling the stairs posed several problems. Figs. 131a & 131b.

145

of handrail height, and supported the rail a few inches above it. (Fig. 131b.) This stair enclosure was made of plywood over a frame of two-by-fours. This unit could easily be removed when necessary by merely taking out half a dozen screws. It was also made in two sections so that one person could lift them. This structure added a certain amount of wall space against which furniture could be placed. It also controlled the draft to some extent and improved the appearance of the room.

In decorating, the stair wall was tied into the rest of the room very simply. The room was given a rough-plastered finish with white Dramex, in the old-time manner, and decorated with a simple stencil border. The stair side, being of wood, was papered in white, and stenciled to match the rest of the room. The wood trim was painted a flat raspberry color.

DINING ROOM INTO KITCHEN

The only room that offered any serious problems in this house was the dining room which we converted into a kitchen. Apart from the normal difficulties of securing an old-time air with modern appliances, traffic from three other rooms to the rear door had to be considered, plus the occasional employment of otherwise waste space for impromptu meals.

This large, square room had a pair of sash windows side by side which did little to dispel the perpetual twilight. The fireplace had been bricked up but the mantel and shelf left in position. There were six doors, including one to the cellar and one to the back yard, cutting every wall into small sections. The biggest problem was to locate the major appliances—stove, sink,

and refrigerator—for the greatest efficiency without undue waste of space. In view of the door locations the only practical solution was to build a peninsula-type counter for the sink, and place the other units against the facing wall, with a door between them. But whatever was done, it would be necessary to move the door of the store room, that was to become a pantry, from its corner location. As it turned out, this door had also to be made narrower. The plan shows the final arrangements.

With the sink, counter, stove and refrigerator forming a compact U-shaped area off which the pantry opened, the meal-preparation area was grouped by itself. This disposed of the traffic problem because it was not necessary to pass through that area to reach the back door from any of the rooms, including the washroom. Ample daylight was provided by replacing the two original windows with a three-section small-paned window incorporating two casements that could be opened by means of a crank. This window was less tall than the units it replaced so that its sill was several inches above the counter.

Since it was impossible to make the old fireplace mantel into a decorative feature, a dropleaf table was fastened below it, hiding the brick-filled opening. On the adjoining wall, a two-foot jog adjacent to the cellar door was put to good use by building in a housekeeper's desk of old pine with a storage cabinet above it. Having a capacious pantry made it unnecessary to install any ceiling-type cabinets, which always detract from the old-time atmosphere.

Since nothing will make white enamel look antique, a major problem here was to subdue the gleaming sink, stove, and re-

How the old dining room became
a usable, efficient kitchen.

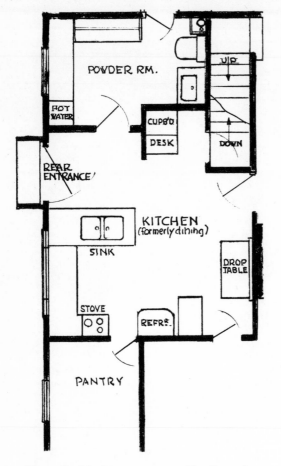

How the kitchen space was distributed.

frigerator. The sink was set into a linoleum-topped pine counter; the stove was crowned with a copper hood containing the exhaust fan; and the refrigerator partly hidden by a small counter with a vertical pine partition up one side of it for tray storage. In this room, the combination of old pine, country-style wallpaper (in the dining area) and gleaming copper produced the simple old-time farmhouse atmosphere that was sought.

A 1790 WRECK

Example Number Two formed a vivid contrast to the 1805 house. Not only because it was a relic of the late 1700s but because of its utter dilapidation. Here was a really unspoiled house that had nothing—no water, plumbing, heat or electricity. An old iron sink and a cast-iron cooking range were the only indoor amenities. Apart from all this, considerable planning was necessary to fit it for modern living. A place had to be found for a kitchen, a washroom, and an upstairs bathroom. How to do all this without destroying the antique air or wrecking the basic structure?

Reduction of the plan to squared paper was the first step, and that brought in the question of where to put the heating plant. Occasional floods and a hillside that drained toward the house had washed tons of dirt through the rear, dry wall of the cellar so that the floor was at a thirty-five degree angle. With that excavated to foundation level, and four inches of concrete spread, the beams would be a scant six feet above the floor. But that is what we did.

To stop further leaks in the back wall, the ground behind the house was graded to slope away from the rear wall. The cellar would now accommodate a specially low-built warm-air furnace. Not having to find a place for that on the main floor, we could plan the rest of the space.

The only stair to the second floor led up from the old kitchen. With its huge fireplace, this room would make a handsome living room. By moving the stair to the front of the house we would have enough room for a kitchen and washroom also. The plan shows how this was done. The stair partition was moved and a section of the rear leanto opened into the space this provided. The result was an L-shaped kitchen and breakfast room that proved ideal.

While this was going on, the masons were reinstating the old kitchen fireplace which was sagging badly. One end of the

The little old farmhouse—a type that so many buy to restore.

eight-foot slab had sunk because of rot in the timber cradle. The beam that supported the cradle also suffered from damp rot and it was considered inadvisable to try and restore the hearth support. Instead, the low end of the stone was jacked up and short brick supporting walls were built out from the chimney base in the cellar. The slab rested firmly on these, and so did the weak beam. Attention could now be paid to the old fireplace lintel which consisted of a four-inch tire iron. This also sagged.

In this fireplace the oven wall was set back a foot into the fireplace so that it gave no support to the lintel. This made it advisable to extend the fireplace cheek out to provide that support. In doing so the appearance of the fireplace would be considerably improved. A brick pillar was therefore built out, separating the oven from the back hearth.

In raising the lintel center, and the brickwork above it, we discovered that a chimney girt had cracked at the chimney breast. The simplest way of remedying this was to insert a post under it. This post was a 6x8-inch timber placed tight against the chimney and resting on one end of the

149

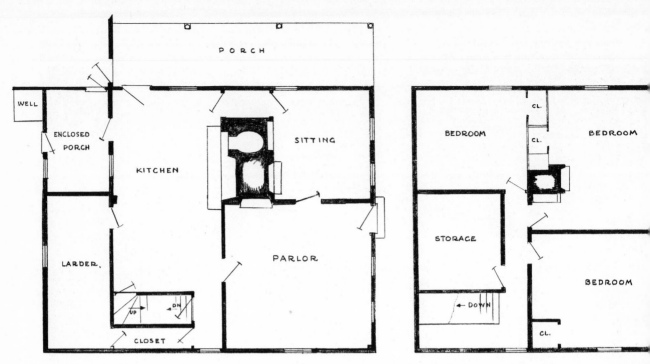

Where to put what—the floor plans reveal the possibilities.

·FIRST FLOOR·

·SECOND FLOOR·

H.L.Williams

150

In the L-shaped kitchen ample space was provided for a breakfast section.

hearthstone. When this post was cased to match the rest of the exposed timbers it not only looked perfectly natural, but served to support one end of a bookcase. The fireplace job was completed by casing the fireplace wall in old pine—using twenty-two-inch pine boards. When given an antique finish these boards looked as though they had been installed when the house was built. Although mantel shelves were used as early as 1727, we did not install one here; the proportions of the fireplace surround seemed too perfect to spoil with a useless addition. And even a six-inch projection would have tended to reduce the apparent width of this already too narrow room. To tie the room together, and provide extra insulation, a dado of wide, horizontal boards was applied to the other three walls.

Two problems were solved by removing a section of the leanto opposite the fireplace. A rear door was provided, opening into the new kitchen, and the new living room was made lighter by installing a large window in the newly exposed outer wall. At the same time a little patio was formed, centering on the old dug well.

The kitchen offered few problems beyond a difference in ceiling heights between the house-proper and the leanto. The leanto ceiling was several inches lower, and the plaster was in bad condition. It was no desecration therefore to tear down the

A battered old kitchen fireplace wall, "before" and "after."

leanto ceiling and raise the ceiling joists. In doing this it was found that the leanto wall had moved outward at some time, so that only the toes of the rafters rested on the plate. This caused the rafter feet to project into the room at the old ceiling level. This was taken care of, and the

rafters properly supported, by running a two-by-six in the new angle between the raised joists and the rafters. This girder rested on the end walls. The space occupied by the girder and the rafter feet was then boxed-in to form a rather interesting jog in the ceiling a foot from the outer wall. The ceiling was insulated before the plastering was done, then the new and old ceilings were matched by means of our Dramex treatment.

One small modern convenience was incorporated by having the built-in telephone desk—which covered the warm-air duct—open to both kitchen and living room. The instrument could be passed through a foot-square opening in the wall, and reached from either side. As will be seen from the plan, the tiny washroom was nicely accommodated beyond the sink end of the kitchen where it tied into the water and drain pipes most efficiently.

The main-floor warm-air ducts and return offered no problem since all distribution was in the cellar. The living-room outlets were concealed by bookcases, and the dining-room and study gratings were let into the closet below the stairs. The second-floor ducts for one bedroom were taken up inside a closet, while the bathroom and second-bedroom ducts had to run up one corner of the dining room and be boxed in. This casing was wallpapered over so that it was not particularly noticeable. To make sure that the wallpaper would stay on, the casing was first papered with newsprint.

In moving the stair to the front of the house, where the main door opened on to it, two rooms were affected. Downstairs, the stair was located on the dining room side of the partition dividing the two front rooms. On the second floor the top of the

open directly into the dining room. All of these operations, it will be noted, resulted in a floor plan that was much more typical of an old-time house than the original one was—and a great deal of waste space was salvaged. The house actually became much more comfortable and convenient without losing any of its colonial air.

The Heart of the House

The heart of an old-time house was the kitchen with its huge fireplace that served for heating as well as cooking and a score of other household chores in days when household necessities were more often made than bought. The room was comparatively large and scantily furnished because of the many activities that were carried on within it besides eating. This applied to small houses in the Southern Colonies as well as the Middle and Northern, though in Virginia proper it later became the practice, where possible, to separate the kitchen from the house.

Window opposite the fireplace was made possible by removing a section of the rear. (*Courtesy Miss Keren Gallowhur*)

stair coincided with the door to the right-hand bedroom. This bedroom no longer needed the doorway because the partition between front and back rooms was removed, making the two into one. A new doorway was made into the left-hand bedroom from the landing because that had lost its original door when the bathroom was installed.

At the foot of the stairs, the front-door frame was heightened to accommodate a four-light transom. This brought daylight into the little hall and made the stairs that much safer. This little entry eliminated the inconvenience of having the front door

The low ceiling of the lean-to was made higher by raising the ceiling joists.

In those days, closet space was extremely limited, and peg-boards and shelves, and an occasional chest, carried everything that could not be placed on the broad hearth or hung from the lintel. Oak, pine, stone or brick, and plaster, with iron utensils, copper vessels and pewter plates combined to make a somewhat cluttered but nevertheless attractive interior. This same combination can be duplicated today.

On the other hand, the modern kitchen cannot be allowed to appropriate one of the most alluring rooms in the house with its cavernous fireplace, worn hearth and battered woodwork. It must be located somewhere else. Where this modern kitchen is put will then depend largely on the equipment to be accommodated and that, in turn, will be governed by the water and power available as much as by individual ideas and needs. In planning any kitchen, therefore, the first thing to be decided is where to put it; the second is what to put in it and where to locate those items, and finally, the type of finish to be used—bare wood or paint, and the degree of formality desired. The logical procedure is to draw a scale plan of the room—half an inch to the foot—and, out of cardboard, cut scale plans of the equipment you are going to use and the furniture or other items that must be accommodated. Even if you do not start out with all the items you want, you may need to plan now so that you will have a place to put them later.

What so many amateur kitchen designers seem to overlook is that an old-time kitchen does not necessarily have to be finished in old pine. Paint can be used in a variety of colors from mustard to Williamsburg blue or Venetian red. Moreover, there is a wide choice of wall colors and patterns from white plaster to patterned wallpapers or even a stencilled border. On the other hand, in seeking the old-time atmosphere we can get considerable help from copper or polished steel, old brass or pewter, and a variety of woods in the form of antique moldings or brackets, aprons, or shelves. Equally important is it to avoid an anachronistic note and cheapening effect of chromium and gaudy plastics.

Wherever possible old-style furniture and open shelves should replace built-in cabinets, especially the ceiling type which affords the most modern touch of all. This is why a pantry is the most useful adjunct of any antique-flavored kitchen where a spacious air demands receding walls.

In the matter of appliance location, the windows of an old house may be a controlling factor. On the other hand, a low window bottom need not interfere with the placing of a counter or sink. In order to preserve the outside appearance of the house, it may be inadvisable to replace a tall window with a short one. In such a case a counter or sink can be placed across the window, either leaving the open pocket, or running a vertical board across the opening to form a trough for the window curtains.

Normally, of course, the windows need to start three or four inches above a counter or sink, and the casement type is much more convenient in this location. Sliding sashes also can be used, but ordinarily they are harder to seal against the weather than the crank-operated casement. Whichever is used, the pane sizes should, of course, match those of the rest of the windows.

Ordinarily, modern appliances do not lend themselves particularly well to the creation of an old-time feel in the kitchen of an antique house. But it is astonishing what can be done with care and study. And old pine is not the sole answer. Quite often the problem is complicated by the fact that you cannot start from scratch in equipping the kitchen. There may be an old sink or a stove that must be kept, and fitted into the scheme; doors and windows badly placed, or plumbing awkwardly located. As a rule, however, most of these drawbacks can be overcome with a little careful planning and manipulation.

A major item in any kitchen is the sink, and its location cannot always be decided at will. The water supply and drain have to be considered. But apart from these factors, there is more latitude than usually realized. For one thing, the sink does not need to be under a window. It can often just as well be at right angles to that source of light. More important is the material of which that sink is composed. Probably the most innocuous, insofar as appearance is concerned, is the stainless-steel sink which goes particularly well with old pine but is no enemy of color and paint. It also tones in well with pewter. But even white enamel can be equally inoffensive if it is of the flat-rimmed type that can be embedded in a cabinet top. So little of the white enamel is then seen from other parts of the room, particularly if it has a stainless-steel holding-down rim. Of course sinks of colored enamel can also be used to fit in with the general decorating scheme.

When the sink already exists, the strategy is to encase it in as much wood as possible. However, it sometimes happens that the best method of dealing with an eyesore or anachronism of this sort is to feature it— emphasize its quaintness and old-fashioned form by designing its surroundings to con-

This refrigerator with its works in the cellar needs no ventilation. (*Courtesy Mr. & Mrs. Frederic C. Jones*)

trast with it. After all, it too represents a bygone day!

If the "eyesore" is an old-fashioned white enamel stove, you may be able to improve its appearance by removing its legs and setting it on a wooden base. It can then be partly hidden by wooden counters that flank it. Behind it you might have a flat sheet of copper reaching up the wall to a copper hood. A somewhat similar treatment can be given a white refrigerator. The floor type, especially if it is of medium size, may be better off for a twelve-inch wooden base in the form of a storage box with a drop front. So long as plenty of ventilation is provided for the mechanism, the box can be partially enclosed. The best method of all in subduing it however is to remove the works to the cellar. Then the box can be totally enclosed in wood, or partially hidden and painted. If the door is flat, it is a simple matter to attach a wooden panel.

Other appliances such as clothes and dish

washers can be obtained in color—or painted with one of the new paints designed for the purpose—and perhaps located under a counter. A good example of this is illustrated.

An old wide-board oak or pine floor can look well in a kitchen, but there are usually wide gaps between them to consider. If these gaps are not filled, as recommended earlier, it may be wise to cover the floor with linoleum or rubber tile. The board floor should be fairly good and level for this. If it is bad, it might better be covered with half-inch plyscord first (a cheap variety of plywood). Ordinarily a floor covering of a solid color should be used, but a spatter-dash pattern may give an old-time air though it does not date before 1840. A much better effect is secured with a stencil pattern. For a narrow kitchen, an all-over pattern will give a better feeling of space than will a border. Kitchen floors hand-stenciled in paint are not recommended—the wear is too great. Elsewhere they are lovely.

In designing wooden counter cabinets there is a primary choice to be made as to style—batten doors or panels? A single board—which is subject to warping—and plywood should not be considered. And nowhere in the house is it more important to subdue the hinges; there are so many of them! Small HL hinges and butterfly hinges are usually appropriate, but on bare wood they need to be of naked iron, not black-japanned; on painted wood they should be painted the same color. Wooden clothes-pin knobs are a pleasant alternative to metal hardware, with invisible spring or ball catches to keep the doors firmly shut.

On Georgian and later houses, moldings can be used more freely; for the simple room the edges of aprons or shelf openings can be curved or even scalloped in restrained patterns.

Much of the kitchen lighting can be from invisible sources. Fluorescent lamps can be hidden behind decorative moldings and under shelves or on top of cabinets. Ordinary light bulbs can be used in fixtures let into the ceiling. If a hanging fixture is called for, the least pretentious is a modern copy of an old whale-oil hanging lamp with its tôle, or tin, shade.

Perhaps more difficult than the kitchen to endow with an antique air is the bathroom. The washbowl, toilet, and bathtub are the uncompromising focal points that challenge the ingenuity. There are two ways of dealing with this problem. One is to go all-out in seeking to disguise these three units; the other is to acknowledge their nec-

A "modern" kitchen at the end of the old keeping room. Fig. 142. (*Courtesy Mr. & Mrs. Fred Baker*)

essary existence and ignore them; building around them an interesting room that will draw attention from them. The latter is the system we favor—and it is the simplest and usually the most satisfactory. In some respects the same philosophy should be applied to kitchens, and the modern equipment overwhelmed by its background and overall design.

In the case of a bathroom, then, here is a chance to create a nicely appointed room with draperies and floor covering to abolish the old-time, blatantly antiseptic atmosphere. The window treatment can be the same as that of any other room. The walls, however, should have some air of impermeability (because of the occasionaly damp atmosphere). A wallpaper of solid color, or, better still, marbleized, would be most effective, with the trim in a contrasting but not too positive color. Painted furniture also might be used—perhaps a table or a dresser and a chair, not too severe in style, to add to the "boudoir" atmosphere without becoming overwhelmingly feminine. A room-size cotton rug would do well here, over a painted or highly waxed original floor.

The lighting fixtures might include a small ceiling lamp with crystal drops, or a star-shaped glass lantern. The table lamp would be of a decorative metal type. This treatment could be varied in detail to cover almost any type of interior from Early Colonial to Greek Revival.

The other method is to use plenty of wood, and enclose all the fixtures as far as possible. This would include a ceiling-high wooden frame to set the bathtub apart and give it the appearance of an old-time built-in alcove bed—without the draperies!

Chapter VIII

Putting a House Together

OF THE large number of houses that are demolished each year, by far the greatest proportion end their existence as scrap building materials in some junk dealer's yard. The availability of such materials at more or less reasonable prices makes it possible for anyone desiring to do so, to reassemble for themselves a complete new-old house made entirely of salvaged beams, panels, hardware and even masonry.

And this building of reproduction houses from old materials is done far more often than may be imagined. Among the ranks of those who consider this procedure worth while are lovers of old houses forced by circumstances to live in an area where no such homes are available, and those who have a feeling for the antique house but prefer to live in one that they know to be sound in every respect, in a location they select, and fully adapted for modern living. At any rate, regardless of the motives, such houses are built from old materials—some utilizing the braced frame, others compromising by assembling the old interiors and exteriors on modern frames of two-by-fours.

Whichever course is adopted, the result can be a house beautiful inside and out that looks as though it had stood on its foundation a century or two. But it will not be cheap!

Most people who undertake this operation first hire an architect and saddle him with the drawing of the plans, the designing of the interior finish, and the producing of the old materials. Finding exactly what is needed may be a long and tedious business, but the results can be extremely worth while. One gentleman of our acquaintance built four houses in this manner, creating for himself an old-time oasis in a growing town, arranging them around a little green complete with babbling brook.

Another friend built a "saltbox" entirely of old materials that more often than once has been mistaken for the local museum—a 17th-Century house close by. Inside, the dull glow of the exquisite pine panelling in the light of candles and log fire completes the illusion of antiquity. Yet at one end of the long keeping-room are the stainless-steel sink and modern appliances so skillfully treated that they seem a natural part of the room.

In all such houses the masonry—fireplaces, hearths, bake ovens, etc.—are built while the house is being put together. Some use any old stone or brick; others salvage old chimneys intact, but if the work is skillfully done the illusion is complete either way.

Painting the stone black gave this stone fireplace and plain pine a more formal air. (*Courtesy Mr. & Mrs. Frederic E. Jones*)

This reproduction of antique houses is, of course, not confined to wooden structures. Where old stone and brick are available, details of the old-time houses can be faithfully reproduced. Stone salvaged from a wrecked house, or even from old stone walls, can be handled so that it gives the appearance of age. Of course the old-style mortar must be used, and the old joints copied, and the finish-pointing done in the authentic local manner. Bricks must be laid in the proper bond and selected for size, degree of crudity, and matching color.

In all cases it seems that the item most difficult to procure is the window sash. Too many of them are damaged or rotted, or of the wrong size or age. But good reproductions of the old sash with wide muntins can readily be had, and when painted will pass casual inspection. But the glass used must ordinarily be much less perfect than new glass.

With a modern foundation and good cellar, such a house, with its slightly irregu-

lar roof, due to the old rafters, and its salvaged trim, can be a delight to the eye. It can also be a snug and comfortable home because everything fits. In planning such a house the greatest difficulty may lie in deciding which type of house or architectural style to choose. One useful guide is the terrain—the site on which the house will stand, and its surroundings.

The "saltbox" is popular but does not offer the most efficient use of indoor space. A Cape Cod or a one and a half story Early American are economical styles in themselves. But sooner or later it may be necessary to make additions, and room arrangements on the second floor may not be satisfactory since one room may have to be entered through another. Then, too, the central chimney, if copied faithfully, may prove much more costly than the end-chimney style. In masonry houses in particular, a thought needs to be given to the future, because alterations and additions may be costly. The safest practice, therefore,

Old pine completely disguises the built-in charcoal grill. (*Courtesy Mr. & Mrs. Frederic E. Jones*)

Using vertical boards or small panels for this overmantel would have necessitated redesigning this room.

is to work out the ultimate plan on paper first. It's cheaper to rub out lines than tear down walls!

Another point to be decided in the planning stage is the period to which the interior must generally conform. Far too many owners incline toward a 1700 date, overlooking the fact that they will want much more comfort than furniture of that period could afford. A slightly pre-Revolutionary date would be much wiser from several standpoints. For one thing, more salvaged materials of that date will be available. For another, there is a much wider range of interior finishes and colors, and a greater variety of exterior and interior trim. To some the idea of making each room represent a different period may be appealing.

One advantage of assembling such a house is that it is possible to have exactly the kind of house you want regardless of period. That is to say, you can select the best of any period to suit your taste, and make the home as ornate or as plain as you wish—and the rooms can be the ideal size for your purpose. But one thing to avoid is haste. If you cannot wait to get just the right materials for your purpose, don't use inferior substitutes. Refuse "seconds" in finishing wood, and above all shun unauthentic knotty pine, and plywood. Plywood can never be disguised, no matter how many coats of paint you apply.

In observing the building of such houses, and noting the problems of finishing the interiors, we have come to the conclusion that the safest procedure is to buy the materials before deciding on interior dimensions. This is particularly important in the matter of ceiling height and wall length where you plan to use panelling or feather-edged boards. If you try to fit a complete wall of old panelling eight feet high and seventeen feet long into a living room seven feet six inches high and sixteen feet long, you will spoil both the woodwork and the room. If that panelling provides an opening three feet six inches high by four feet six inches wide for the fireplace, you will need to do some juggling to make it fit. Likewise old floorboards should not have to be pieced out. These are but two of the many details that will make all the difference between a convincing reproduction and an obvious fake. And sincerity is the first essential for interior and exterior alike.

One important point in building a new house from old materials is that you can arrange the rooms to suit yourself. You do not have to adhere strictly to old-time plans,

160

No one would guess that this lovely old house was not built 200 years ago on its present site. (*Courtesy Mr. & Mrs. Fred Baker*)

and the interior will look even better than one that has been drastically remodelled. One of the major headaches in modernizing any old house has always been the location of an upstairs bathroom. Quite often that means either a waste of space, inaccessibility, or the need for passing through an-

other room to reach it. In one old house that we took over for remodeling, the bathroom was in a wing, tucked in the corner of what had been a small bedroom. Not only was that bedroom rendered useless but one other back bedroom became an oversized passageway. What had been a four-bedroom house now had only two. Where more than one upstairs bathroom is required, the problem becomes that much more acute. But in ignoring the old-time floor plans in building *de novo,* all of the benefits and none of the drawbacks can be achieved.

Another point to be considered in planning such a house is the choice of frame. We have never been too enthusiastic about building a reproduction on a modern balloon frame. This introduces problems in reproducing the old-time corner posts and beams which usually are faked. Building the house of the large timbers in the first place would avoid that, and result in a more authentic reproduction. Furthermore, with modern equipment and methods, the job can be done quickly and efficiently. There will be no need to gather the neighbors together for an old-time "raisin' bee." As in the case of the old house we showed earlier that was taken apart and moved, a crane lifts the timbers and holds them while they are being pegged together. The only requisite is that timbers of the proper length be obtained in the first place. If the parts of the house are bought ahead of time, as we suggest, and matched as far as possible, there will be no problem here.

Of course, these problems do not arise to the same extent with masonry buildings. But even then there is need to acquire horizontal timbers suitable as to length, and to see that, if they are already notched for joists, etc., they will not be dangerously weakened by further cutting.

In these pages we are able to show some particularly successful recreations of Colonial houses built from materials one hundred to two hundred years old. The first of

Triple windows give added light.

these is the handsome "saltbox" mentioned before, with a pilastered chimney behind the ridge, and a 1720 façade. Even the clapboard siding is from an antique house, and still unpainted. Skillful landscaping has achieved a natural setting, lovely in its simplicity, that might be as old as the house is supposed to be. The chimney is of stone, topped with brick, the drip-course cleverly concealing the flashing.

Because this "saltbox," like all others, has rear windows that permit too little light to enter the old kitchen, triple windows were installed. These consist of three old sashes, each having twelve lights over eight, making the room livable without detracting from its antique air. This emphasizes a point that we have made before; that practically every old house will incorporate some evidence of change and growth, and be the better for it. And be all the more convincing as an antique. Extreme purity of design is not always desirable in a house

162

to be lived in.

The roof of this house is covered with hand-split wood shingles, naturally weathered. The interior of the house is equally authentic, employing a great deal of natural old pine, with exquisite examples of early paneling on each fireplace wall. The fireplaces and hearths themselves are careful reproductions with old brick for parlor and bedroom, and squared stone for the kitchen. Strict attention was paid to the size of the joints, the color of the mortar, and the pointing.

In the old hall, the fireplace surround is finished with a simple bolection molding, topped and framed by a particularly fine example of raised panelling. The end walls are covered with rather narrow feather-edged boarding that, because of its proportions, tends to increase the apparent height of the room.

In the old kitchen, now a living room, the hearth is of stone and this goes particularly well with the massive exposed timbers, and the twenty-inch-wide old vee-jointed pine boards over the rudimentary mantel. At one end of this large room, and separated from the rest of it by a wide fireside settle, is the modern kitchen. (Fig. 142.) Unfortunately the picture does not do justice to the unobtrusive, sand-colored appliances and the stainless-steel sink which tone in so well with the old wood. The sink is set beneath another double-sash window and is adequately illuminated after dark by a light recessed in the ceiling and practically unnoticeable. With carefully chosen antique furniture and accessories, this house has all the "feel" as well as the appearance of a pure, early 18th-Century house of charm and distinction. (Fig. 147.)

Careful reproduction gives this living room an entirely authentic appearance. (*Courtesy Mr. & Mrs. Fred Baker*)

The second reproduction represents a house of somewhat less formal character, more of the farmhouse type, with that true old-time home atmosphere that is a perfect setting for its informal, antique furniture and fittings. Here there is no casing of timbers, because the beams and posts, made to be exposed, bear the marks of careful working with old-time tools. A great deal of pine is used here also, but the interior doors are of the four-panel type with HL hinges, except for the closets which have batten doors. The only decorative feature of the interior is a built-in corner cupboard with open shelves. Wide boarding and nicely modelled gunstock posts, peg boards, and candle shelves give the rooms character.

In this house all ceiling beams are exposed, and the upstairs floors made double, with heavy building paper between the two layers of old boards, the underneath ones of which form the first-floor ceilings.

The keeping room fireplace carefully reproduced. (*Courtesy Mr. & Mrs. Fred Baker*)

A less formal interior with a true old-time feel. (*Courtesy Mr. & Mrs. Frederic E. Jones*) Fig. 149.

Assembling the Old Materials

What you haven't got in the way of materials you can usually buy if you look far enough. Wreckers and junk yards often have old doors and windows, beams and hardware—even clapboard siding to patch the exterior where that leanto came off! Then there are local historical societies that salvage such material, particularly doors and architraves, and sometimes have excess pieces they are glad to dispose of to swell their funds for restorations. There are also house-restoration firms and individuals who collect these things. From them—and sometimes as a result of a newspaper advertisement—you can procure panelling for a complete wall, usually the fireplace side, or for a dado or wainscot. Then there are woodworkers who will make up the panelling from old wood to order—a simple job, given the proper tools and the knowhow! Just be sure they match the old-time molding shapes! Finally, there are dilapidated houses that still have timbers and trim worth saving. Find the owner and make a deal—he may be anxious to realize what he can on them.

As regards ironwork, a friend in need may be the old village blacksmith; there are quite a few of them left who can duplicate the old hardware. But make sure he uses old techniques and doesn't think antiquing merely consists of random hammer marks or a lopsided pattern. One thing to avoid is the use of modern imitations of old-time hand-forged nails; nothing is more obvious!

About the hardest thing to replace is the old glass. Besides being thin and wavy, it is extremely brittle, and almost impossible to cut. One prolific source of old glass is old picture frames—thinner than window glass and needing therefore great care when installing. While it may be easy to remove old glass if the putty has broken away, it takes both skill and care to replace it. The back putty must be especially soft so that the glass does not need to be pressed too hard in bedding it. Pressure in any one spot will crack it in an instant.

The best place to find very old brick is in the country. In driving around, a sharp watch is kept for signs of an old house either falling down or having been burnt. Such bricks can be salvaged if great care is taken in removing them from a chimney base or wall. But it will pay to find the owner and get his permission before you start to take the relic apart. We have never yet been refused.

Such bricks are usually brittle, but the lime mortar will be fairly soft so that the bricks are not hard to clean. The thick mortar can be knocked off with a trowel, and the remnants scraped off with a putty knife. If a brick is hard, it may help to soak it in water, but if the brick is soft and clayey, soaking will do more harm than good. The bricks will not break so easily if they are firmly supported throughout their length while being cleaned. All of these bricks can be cut with a circular saw made for the job, or with a hacksaw. Usually, however, the best way to cut them is to notch them all around with the edge of a trowel then break them off with a sharp blow.

All except the glassy, burned bricks can be sanded to shape, but this is not recommended for the exposed ends. If the bricks are used for hearths, or other places where a smooth surface is required, a drum-type sander can be used to take off the high spots. One or two coats of thin orange shellac (half alcohol) will seal them and tone down the sanded surface.

In some of the more formal fireplaces, particularly those in bedchambers, the brick surround can be given a coat of sand-and-lime plaster. When set—and assuming that the surface is quite smooth—this plaster can be painted either a dull white or a dead black. Special paints are made for the purpose. It is equally simple to attach ceramic tiles around the opening in a bed of plaster-of-paris.

On the whole, the reproduction of an antique house differs only in degree from the rebuilding of a house that has been entirely taken apart and moved. In trying to assemble a new-old house, the principal problem is finding parts that will go together, and fit in a predetermined pattern as a unified whole as is done when new parts are used. There is always a great deal of cutting and fitting to be done, but that can be minimized by making a careful list of timbers, flooring, panelling, doors, and windows of specified types and dimensions. The alternative method of building piecemeal and hoping to get parts to fit later, we do not recommend. That way lies frustration.

The fireplace wall of the room in Fig. 149. (*Courtesy Mr. & Mrs. Frederic E. Jones*)

Chapter IX

Moving Old Houses

IN THESE days of violent expansion and ruthless progress, when land values are doubled and trebled in short order, when farms are transformed overnight into suburban developments and country villages blossom into "bedroom" communities for some mushrooming town twenty miles away, many an antique house is condemned to demolition. When this happens it is usually the professional house wrecker who does the job—for the value of the materials plus a fee of five hundred to one thousand dollars from the owner of the land, on the understanding that the site is cleared and levelled. But there are exceptions.

It sometimes happens that a private individual, hearing that a certain old house is to be torn down, makes the owner a cash offer—and so secures for himself a home for one-twentieth to one-fortieth of what it would cost to build. His only problem then is to move the house to where he wants it— a hundred yards or two hundred miles—and one can cost as much as the other!

Happily enough, this transporting of a house from one site or neighborhood to another can very often prove not only worth while but highly profitable both in terms of investment and aesthetic satisfaction. Sometimes the house can be moved *in toto*, com-plete with chimneys and fireplaces, without even taking the pictures off the wall. Under other circumstances, the house must be taken apart and moved in sizable chunks; or it may even have to be entirely disassembled and rebuilt, stone by stone or timber by timber. Whichever system is used, the results can be much the same from an observer's point of view—the house on its new foundations may look as though it had been erected there generations before.

The method to be employed in moving any antique house will depend upon a great deal more than the whim of the owner. The size and shape of the house, its construction, the terrain to be traversed, the obstacles to be encountered, the distance, and above all the cost of permissions, all need to be considered. Moving any house is a minor miracle of engineering, and moving an *antique* house whether of wood or masonry calls not only for skill and experience but for understanding and a feeling for the old structure and what it represents to its owner. Such a mover will go to great lengths to avoid damage to the original parts and materials, and salvage everything possible—even the cellar walls if necessary.

In moving a house that is to be restored and not merely remodelled, even the origi-

Moving an antique house. Here is a 1740 gem being saved from demolition! (*Courtesy Mr. & Mrs. Richard D. Wolf*)

Picking up the house to set it on rollers. (*Courtesy Mr. & Mrs. Harrold DeGroff*)

Transferring a house from the trailer calls for perfect leveling. (*Courtesy Mr. & Mrs. Harrold DeGroff*)

nal foundation stones and chimney bases are of importance. This is, of course, an expensive complication that is not required when the house is to be revamped for modern living.

Moving in One Piece

The simplest method of moving a house is to jack it up and put it on a trailer. That process, however, is nowhere so simple as it sounds. Before an antique house can be jacked up, huge timbers or "needles" must be placed under it, each in its correct position to carry its share of the load. This means that holes must be cut in the foundation walls and through cellar walls or partitions. If there is no cellar, or only a partial one, this becomes a complicated job. Then some of the ground under the house must be excavated to let the needles pass under the sills and beams; to allow for jacks being positioned, and to cut through the chimney bases. Digging a cellar underneath a house cannot be done with a steam shovel —it calls for spade work and muscle, and plenty of time. Such a consideration may even make the project too costly. Luckily quite often it does not. Finally, the phone and power lines must be disconnected, the water supply, heating pipes, and plumbing cut off at floor level. In the case of a large house, or one with a number of appendages, the porches, ells, and extensions will probably have to be cut off and moved separately.

Once the needles are in place, jacks can be inserted under them, and the ticklish job of lifting the whole house begins. This has to be done gently and slowly, with the house kept on an even keel. Each jack is turned a precise amount at the same instant on a whistled signal and, inch by inch,

the structure is lifted. More timbers are inserted, and the jacking repeated till the house is several feet in the air, so that the low-slung trailer or trailers can be backed into position. These trailers are made of steel girders with sixteen to twenty-four small but sturdy wheels. The trailer trucks that pull them have fifteen gears so that they can start without shock and move at a snail's pace, smoothly and evenly.

Now the house is on its way, but if it is to cross or travel on a highway, a great deal of preliminary work will have been done long before. Permits must have been obtained from highway and police departments, for the road must not be damaged or the traffic snarled. The whole route the house will take must have been surveyed by the mover to see what obstacles must be removed. Almost certainly power and telephone lines will have to be raised or cut temporarily; the bus company may have to be consulted, and the consent of property owners en route asked to lop branches of trees.

Naturally, all of these things have to be taken into account in estimating the total cost—a job for the owner himself. Sometimes expense can be saved by removing the house chimney to ridge level and rebuilding it again. Apart from the substantial bond usually required by State highway departments to cover damage to roads, sewers, water mains, and bridges, the power and phone line work can account for the major parts of these costs. On one two-story wooden house that we contemplated moving a mere two blocks, the cost of raising the wires alone was $1,300!

Not all houses, of course, need this full treatment. A small house, or one being transported only a short distance, can often

With modern moving methods house and chimney can be transferred long distances with the pictures still on the wall. (*Courtesy Mr. & Mrs. Richard D. Wolf*)

Precision methods are called for. (*Courtesy Mr. & Mrs. Richard D. Wolf*)

Setting the house down on its new foundation is a slow, ticklish job! (*Courtesy Mr. & Mrs. Harrold DeGroff*)

be moved on rollers at comparatively little cost.

House Surgery

Another method of moving a house that has certain advantages, is the sectional system. This entails cutting the house vertically into two or more parts, and perhaps horizontally at floor or roof level, or both. Half a house is much easier to haul along a highway than a whole one, and so is a roof folded flat and stood on edge. This method is limited to houses of wood. Drawings are first made and photographs taken to ensure proper replacement of every single unit. To aid in re-construction, every piece is numbered. The usual practice is to demolish the chimney and rebuild it with as many of the same bricks or stones as can be salvaged. The house sections are transported on large flat trucks. The old oak, time-hardened tree nails (the wooden pegs) must be drilled out of their holes.

When moving a house by this method some damage must be expected. Old dry plaster will not stand vibration and usually some replastering of walls will be necessary, especially where the plaster was in poor condition to begin with. Otherwise, properly done, a flaking job will not even crack a window pane. When a house is cut through the middle in this fashion the ridge pole (if there is one), the plates, and the sills are severed. On reassembling the house an extra rafter is inserted next to the one along which the cut was made, and the two are bolted together. The rest of the cut timbers are strongly joined by bolted metal plates or wood stiffeners. With this method all chimneys are best rebuilt. This affords an opportunity for lining the chimney for safety's sake. Every precaution must be taken to see that the fireplaces are reproduced as they were. This means that practically every brick should be marked so that it finds its proper place. It is unfortunate that many of the old bricks crumble when being taken apart. They should be handled with care. Most movers who specialize in handling very old houses retain bricklayers and masons who can copy old work, and what's more, are willing to do so. We have seen such jobs in which the trowel work and color of the mortar made it impossible to tell in what century the work was done.

The mover will also replace roof shingles in such a way that no trace of the cut remains. By removing odd ones along the line of the roof separation, detection is impossible. Of course, porches, steps, and small additions are first taken off when this method of house removal is employed.

On page 171 is a picture of a Cape Cod type of house that was moved from its native New Hampshire to lower Massachu-

An old Cape Cod being taken apart for moving 150 miles.
(*Courtesy Mrs. Nelson Fay*)

With every piece numbered the house is quickly reassembled
with the help of modern equipment. (*Courtesy Mrs. Nelson Fay*)

Restored to its former glory the old house takes on a new
lease of life in another State. (*Courtesy Mrs. Nelson Fay*)

setts by dismantling the entire structure
and then re-erecting it. This illustrates the
fourth method of house moving. The usual
system is first to have a complete set of
architectural drawings made that include
every dimension. Then a complete set of
exterior and interior photographs must be
compiled. This entails a great deal of preliminary work. Because of this, and the
enormous amount of labor involved in this
method of house moving, the cost is high.
The house has to be entirely rebuilt, and
old materials used to replace those damaged
or destroyed.

With this system, the siding and roofing
are first removed, and as the timbers become exposed they must be marked, using
a different colored paint for each section or
group. The marks must consist of identifying numbers, and these numbers, in their

proper color, must be placed on the drawings. The roof shingles of course cannot be
saved, but sometimes clapboards can be re-
used. Since the old-time, hand-made nails
cannot always be removed from the clapboards, they have to be knocked through,
or clipped. Similar detailed care has to be
given the fireplaces and the bake oven, as
well as the timbers that are let into the
masonry.

In a house that has to be taken apart in
this manner, there is an excellent opportunity for applying the proper kind of insulation, of installing electric wiring, modern
heating, and plumbing. It is also possible to
replace or splice any rotted or damaged timber, and to square joints, so that a perfectly
constructed house, sound in every detail,
results.

Chapter X

The Jewel and the Setting

Let there be adjoining the House a convenient garden, it being the purest of human pleasures, and a great refreshment to the Spirit of Man without which Buildings are but gross Handyworks.
—Primatt

In putting any antique house together in a new location, the setting should be an important consideration. Lawns, trees, and plantings can give the plainest old house distinction and interest, but in planning such a background there is no rough-and-ready formula; you have to know what you are doing! And that means study. Here are half a dozen old houses of various types that have gained in loveliness with flowers and foliage hiding foundations, emphasizing their better features, altering their apparent proportions, and framing their doors and windows with creepers that add color and soften harsh lines.

The first of these illustrates the values of eliminating that ever-ugly feature of an ell —the porch floor. Near the porch, and parallel with it, is a low drop-fence—a wall of stone that permits of raising a section of the lawn high enough to cover the foundations. An old-style fence raises the level of vision from the lane, and a creeper softens the edges of the delicate arches of the

porch roof. At the house gable, denser foliage and a tree provide a measure of privacy in a sheltered corner of this miniature paradise.

In the second view, the kitchen door of this 1740 Early Georgian opens onto a sun-trap ringed with tall trees and flowering bushes. Bird-feeding stations adorn the trees flanking the little terrace, and nearby are shade trees under which the chaise-longue is stretched and tea is served. In the foreground is a low wall smothered in candytuft, Jacob's ladder, primroses, and lupins, that rings the sunny space invisible from the road or neighbors' gardens.

Equally lovely is the little gambrel-roofed house whose dooryard is sheltered by the one and a half story, creeper-clad ell. The deep red of the buildings, and the cool gold of the stone terrace are a wonderful foil for the clustered rose bushes that soon will be a mass of yellow blooms, and the clumps of irises that sparkle in the sun. The rolling turf wandering among these beds offers many an enticing spot for sun-bathing and relaxation. Try to imagine this old house rising starkly from the bare, flat ground!

On hilly ground and bedrock at surface level, high foundations are inescapable and

(Courtesy Mr. & Mrs. Laurence Fellows)

(Courtesy Mrs. Russell P. Haidet)

(Courtesy Mr. & Mrs. Charles K. Dodge)

(Courtesy Mr. & Mrs. Shailer Dow)

(Courtesy Mr. & Mrs. Robert I. Carter)

pose special problems. In the fourth picture, the tall stone steps and iron rail decree a slightly more formal planting. Here clumps of box and yew, nestling in a bed of pachysandra, that separate a flagstone path from the lawn, defy the steep slope to form a solid foundation for the little house perched so primly on its knoll. A flowery creeper provides a splash of color alongside the inviting doorway, and affords dynamic balance to the slightly offset dormer above.

In the last of these peeps into fairyland, hillside plantings with creepers over old stumps and a lacy pattern of leaves in the sunshine perfectly complement the cool shade of an open porch facing the old shed-topped well. And how much the little house, with its formal, classic touches, owes to its backdrop of ancient elms and butternuts and maples!

All of these are homes—old American houses restored, and remodelled or otherwise preserved from decay and dissolution by owners who have recognized that as a happy heart and a shining face go together, so do a house and its garden.

176

Glossary

ARCHITRAVE—in classical architecture, the lowermost division of an entablature. Any ornamented band or molding carried around a door or window opening.

ASHLAR—squared and faced building stone. If the sizes of the blocks vary it is called random ashlar.

BALUSTER—an upright support of a handrail. "Banister" is a colloquial form of "baluster."

BALUSTRADE—a row of balusters carrying a rail.

BATTEN—a board fastened across two or more others to hold them together.

BEAD—a convex, rounded molding, usually semicircular in section.

BEAM IRON—an iron bolt used to hold a wood beam tight to a masonry wall.

BEEHIVE OVEN—An external bake oven, shaped like a circular beehive.

BOLECTION—a molding which projects beyond the general surface of a panel or connects two surface levels.

BONDING—in bricks or stonework, the binding of the pieces together by overlapping lengthwise and in thickness.

BORNING ROOM—a main-floor room at the warm end of a house reserved for births because of its proximity to the kitchen fireplace and the source of hot water.

BRACED FRAME—a house frame of massive timbers, jointed and pegged together, and supporting small timbers to which the walls and floors are fastened.

BUTT—(a) the hinged edge of a door, (b) a hinge applied to the edge or butt of a door.

BUTTERY—a cool room used as a larder or pantry.

CARRIER—the main support of a stair formed by cutting out a heavy plank for the attachment of treads and risers.

CATSLIDE—the long rear roof of a leanto house (Southern). The house itself.

CELLAR GIRT—one of the braced-frame timbers extending from front to rear sill alongside a chimney in the cellar ceiling.

CHIMNEY POST—one of the posts of a braced frame adjacent to the chimney.

CHRISTIAN DOOR—any door whose stiles and rails form a cross, particularly with the X-shape stiles in a lower panel.

CHAMFER—a flat surface formed by cutting away a corner, edge, or arris.

CLINCH—to bend over and hammer down the protruding point of a nail so that it cannot be withdrawn.

CORNER BOARD—a vertical board nailed over the corner post of a braced-frame house.

CORBEL—a supporting projection on the face of a wall. Stepped bricks or stones arranged to support something.

COUNTERSINK—to chamfer the edges of a hole so that a screw head will not project above the surface.

COURSE—a horizontal row of bricks, stones, shingles, etc.

CRADLE—a rubble-filled, wood structure that supports a main-floor hearthstone.

CRUCKS—Pairs of bent, tree timbers crossed at the top to support a ridge pole in house framing.

DENTIL—a small, rectangular block forming one of a series applied as an ornament.

DEPENDENCY—any building separate from a house it is designed to serve, such as a separate kitchen or servant's quarters.

DOCKED CHIMNEY—a short chimney resting on a house-frame timber or other support, usually close under a roof.

DRIP COURSE—a projecting course of masonry to deflect rainwater from a wall or structural joint beneath it.

DUTCH KICK—the tilt of the eaves in a pitched-roof house, typical of Dutch and Flemish architecture.

DUTCH OVEN—(a) a shallow, iron kettle for baking, with a tightfitting rimmed cover to hold burning coals; (b) a tin oven of the reflecting type for roasting before an open fire.

ENTABLATURE—the architrave, frieze, and cornice resting on the capitals of columns or analogous parts in post-and-lintel construction.

ENTASIS—a slight convex curvature given to the taper of a column to make the sides appear as straight lines.

FEATHER EDGE—a board trimmed to a fine edge to fit into the groove in another board.

FENESTRATION—the arrangement and proportioning of windows.

FIRE FRAME—an iron frame set into fireplace to reduce its size and contain the fire.

FRAMED OVERHANG—a floor overhanging the one below it because of the upper floor horizontal timbers extending beyond the vertical face of the floor below.

FRANKLIN STOVE—a metal fireplace connected to a chimney by a funnel or pipe so as to bring the fire out into the room to conserve heat.

FURRING—a light framework applied to walls, ceilings, floors, etc. to support boards, plaster, or other finish surface.

GAMBREL ROOF—a form of curb roof, the lower part being at a steeper angle than the upper part.

GIRT—a horizontal beam framed into the posts of a braced-frame house at floor level; may be front, rear, chimney, cellar, or end girt.

GUDGEON—a hook on which a hinge turns—also called a pintle.

HALF-LAPPED—a joint formed by cutting away two boards or timbers where they cross so that they fit together in the thickness of one timber.

HALF-TIMBERED FRAME—a house frame constructed of heavy timbers divided horizontally to form spaces which are filled with bricks, plaster, etc. constituting exterior walls.

HEADER—a brick laid so that its shorter face, or head, shows in the surface of a wall.

HEWN OVERHANG—a floor overhanging the wall below it because of the lower vertical timbers being cut back.

JOIST—any small timber laid horizontally to support a floor or ceiling.

KEEPING-ROOM—the old-time name for the living room or common room.

KING-POST—the vertical post of a roof truss consisting of a ceiling joist, a pair of rafters, with the vertical post resting on the joist and extending upward to the junction of the rafters.

LEANTO HOUSE—a house with a rear shed addition whose roof is a continuation of the house roof forming one long slope. A cat-slide house or "saltbox."

LINTEL—a horizontal member spanning an opening.

MANTEL—the woodwork around a fireplace.

MORTISE—(a) a rectangular hole into which is fitted a solid piece of the same shape, called a tenon, to form a mortise-and-tenon joint; (b) a similar hole cut in a door stile to receive a mortise lock.

MULLION—a vertical bar or pier between windows.

MUNTIN—a small, slender mullion forming a sash bar to hold the glass in a window.

OUTSHOT—any structure attached to a house to increase its useful space.

PALLADIAN WINDOW—a group of three windows, the center one being higher and having a rounded top, named after its inventor Andrea Palladio, 16th-Century architect.

PEDIMENT—the triangular space forming a roof gable or similar treatment used over doors and windows, etc. Variations include the broken, and scroll types.

PENDILLS—carved drops formed at the lower ends of second-floor posts in a framed overhang.

PIE STEPS—steps of a stair triangular in shape so as to carry the stair around an angle.

PINTLE—a pin or hook on which a strap hinge swings.

PLATE—the horizontal wooden members that lie on top of a wall or form the topmost horizontal members of a braced frame that support the roof rafters.

PORCH—(a) a covered entrance either inside or outside the front door of a house; (b) any covered enclosure or veranda attached to the house.

PURLIN—a horizontal roof member supporting rafters, usually at their middles.

QUEEN-POST—one of a pair of vertical members of a roof truss consisting of a pair of rafters resting on a joist, the queen posts extending upward from the joist to the junction of the rafters with a tie-beam.

RABBET—a right-angle groove cut in the edge of a board or other materials.

RAKE—the slope of a roof or the verge board that follows the rake.

RIDGE BOARD—a board placed vertically between the top ends of rafters to form a roof ridge.

RISING HINGE—a butt-type hinge, one half of which moves vertically in relation to the other as it opens.

ROOFTREE—the ridge pole; topmost member of a roof frame.

RUBBLE—rough, broken stone or brick.

SILL—(a) the bottommost horizontal timber of a wall; (b) the exterior horizontal member on which a window frame rests.

SINK—a recess or depression.

SMOKE CHAMBER—a boxlike structure attached to a chimney flue and in which wood can be burned for the purpose of smoking meats.

179

SPLINE—or Loose Tongue; a thin strip of wood placed in the grooves in the edges of two adjoining boards to form a joint.

STILE—an upright member in framing or paneling.

STRAP HINGE—a hinge composed of two leaves, one fastened to the frame, the other to the door. The common name for a pintle-strap hinge.

STRETCHER—a brick laid lengthwise in a wall.

STRINGER—a side member of a staircase against which the steps abut.

STUD—a light, vertical member in a house frame to which interior and exterior coverings are applied.

SUMMER—or Bressummer; a principal floor timber or beam.

TENON—the end of a rail or beam cut to form a projection that fits into a corresponding hole, or mortise, in another piece.

TIE-BEAM—a horizontal beam extending between a pair of roof rafters to prevent them bending inwards or spreading at the feet. Also called a windbeam.

TRAMMEL—an adjustable iron hook for hanging pots over a fire.

TREE-NAIL—a wooden pin used for securing tenon and lap joints in a timber frame.

VERGE BOARD—a board or molding covering the end rafter in a gable.

WEATHERBOARD—a clapboard.

WIND BEAM—a roof tie-beam. q.v.

Index

C

Cape Cod house
  characteristics, 67-68
  floor plan, 67, 68
  half-house, 67
  origin, 57, 67
  stair location, 67, 68
  windows, 68
Casing, 28, 113, 152
Captain's walk, 76
"Catslide," 57, 73, 74
Ceiling, 27
Cellar, 27, 74, 102, 123
Central-chimney house, 47-49
  Cape Cod type, 67-68
  chimney construction, 47
  Early American type, 27, 57, 65-66
  fireplaces, 47
  floor plan, 47
  origin, 57
  oven, 47
  purpose, 47
  "saltbox," 57-65
Chair rail, 90, 97
Chamber, 54, 61, 66
Chamfer, 96, 98, 113
Chester County, 43
Chimney
  adding new, 132
  arch, 47
  brick, 41
  construction, 46, 47-48, 49, 72, 74
  "docked," 50-51
  drip course, 50
  end, 41, 45, 46, 72
  fire hazards, 50
  flashing, 50
  girts, 27, 49
  leaking, 50
  locations, 41, 49, 50, 51, 60, 87
  ovens, 51-52
  pilastered, 50, 163
  posts, 27, 28, 32
  rebuilding, 131
  repairing, 123-25
  shapes, 50, 72
  size, 27, 72, 74

  stone, 27
  vault, 47
Clapboards, 25, 33-34, 74
  aid in dating, 99
  beaded, 33, 35
  early, 33
  featheredge, 33
  graduating, 34, 99
  how used, 33
  mitered, 34
  paint under, 115
  shadow line, 35
  size, 33, 99
  wooden, 33, 99
Clay, 47, 50
Clemence House, 34
Closets, 102
Collar beam, 24, 36, 37
Connecticut, 41, 87, 100
Corbels, 44, 52, 72, 119
Corner boards, 33
Corner braces, 24, 25, 37
Corner cupboards, 63, 79
Corner posts, 24, 36
Cornice, 74, 81, 95
Cradle, 49
Cruck construction, 22-23
Curved braces, 24
Cusps, 106, 109

D

Dado, 79
Date panel, 87, 97, 99
Dating houses, 57-65, 85-87
  by clapboards, 99
  by documentary evidence, 41, 85-87
  by doors, 93-96, 97
  by extensions, 68-69
  by floor boards, 116-18
  by hardware, 102-07, 116
  by nails, 101, 116
  by panelling, 97-99
  by windows, 90
Delaware, 79, 99, 100
Dentils, 74
Documentary evidence, 41, 85-87

189